ROUTLEDGE LIBRARY EDITIONS:
EPISTEMOLOGY

Volume 2

SCEPTICISM AND THE FIRST PERSON

SCEPTICISM AND THE FIRST PERSON

S. COVAL

Routledge
Taylor & Francis Group
LONDON AND NEW YORK

First published in 1966

This edition first published in 2015
by Routledge
2 Park Square, Milton Park, Abingdon, Oxon OX14 4RN

and by Routledge
711 Third Avenue, New York, NY 10017

Routledge is an imprint of the Taylor & Francis Group, an informa business

British Library Cataloguing in Publication Data
A catalogue record for this book is available from the British Library

ISBN: 978-1-138-80196-7 (Set)
ISBN: 978-1-315-69475-7 (Set) (ebk)
ISBN: 978-1-138-90806-2 (Volume 2) (hbk)
ISBN: 978-1-138-90870-3 (Volume 2) (pbk)
ISBN: 978-1-315-69472-6 (Volume 2) (ebk)

Publisher's Note
The publisher has gone to great lengths to ensure the quality of this reprint but points out that some imperfections in the original copies may be apparent.

Disclaimer
The publisher has made every effort to trace copyright holders and would welcome correspondence from those they have been unable to trace.

SCEPTICISM
and the First Person

S. COVAL

METHUEN & CO LTD

First published 1966 by Methuen & Co. Ltd.
11 New Fetter Lane
London EC4

Printed in Great Britain
by Ebenezer Baylis and Son, Ltd
The Trinity Press, Worcester, and London

Acknowledgments

I should like to thank Professor A. J. Ayer and Mr P. F. Strawson for their help and opposition. It will be frequently obvious where I am indebted to them. John Baker, D. Daniels and David Wiggins read this work in manuscript and made many useful suggestions.

To M, S & T

Contents

INTRODUCTION page ix

ABSTRACT xiii

I. THE *A PRIORI* DEADLOCK 1

1 *Are pronoun differences or similarities to be dominant?*
2 *The argument from necessary plurals which seems to settle the issue*
3 *The argument from necessary plurals is indecisive as regards two possibilities*
4 *An argument against the view that personal demonstratives are extrudable*
5 *Does a personal particular help?*
6 *Some arguments for and against personal uniqueness*
7 *The present state of the argument*

II. PERSONAL PRONOUNS A 21

8 *Four things pursued*
9 *Special features of the first person*
10 *Are the special features of the first person needed for the performance of self-reference?*
11 *Are the personal pronouns essential to the formulation of the paradoxes?*
12 *The function and importance of the special features of the first person*
13 *The systematically elusive 'I'*

III. PERSONAL PRONOUNS B 39

14 *Which of the special features of the first person are essential to self-reference?*
15 *Reference and self-reference.*
16 *Is our view of the first person relevant to the alleviation of the paradoxes?*

17 *Speaker-hearer asymmetry*
18 *Symmetrical asymmetry among all three persons*

IV. PRIVATE LANGUAGE 63
19 *Systematically private language*
20 *The necessity of the first person to private language*
21 *Arguments not to be used*
22 *The relevant nature of first person asymmetry*
23 *Self-individuation pre-supposes non-self-individuation*
24 *The first person overburdens private language*

V. EPISTEMOLOGY A 71
25 *An undercutting question*
26 *Speech as action and its implications for the sceptic*
27 *Systematically ulterior motives*
28 *The sceptical position denies its own presuppositions*

VI. EPISTEMOLOGY B 83
29 *Unhelpful answers to 'How do you know you are X?'*
30 *Feeling*
31 *Tactual and non-tactual feelings*
32 *Non-tactual feelings and the other senses*
33 *Corrigibility*

VII. SELF-ASCRIPTION AND OTHER ASCRIPTION 101
34 *Material self-ascription and personal self-ascription*
35 *Non-transferability*
36 *P-claims, M-claims and sufficiently similar circumstances*

SELECTED BIBLIOGRAPHY 115

Introduction

It may help as an introduction to characterize some main competing positions and to show where the views argued here are related to such issues as were raised by Ryle, Wittgenstein, Strawson, and Place and Smart.

Suppose it was Ryle's position, in *The Concept of Mind*, that mental epithets are distinguished from material epithets by their dispositional character. If asked whether there are material predicates *and* mental predicates Ryle would, strictly speaking, reply that there were not both. He would say so because he believes that, in the last analysis, certain paradoxes of selves and others would otherwise result. Apparently the only way to close successfully the epistemological gap between selves and others, to avoid the paradoxes of such a dualism, is to limit the involved terms to one or other side of the gap – in Ryle's case the 'others'' side.

Opting for one side or other of the gap, under pressure from paradox, is typical of most, if not all, approaches to the problems of selves and others and selves and things. Even Wittgenstein exhibited the standard reaction to such pressure with his claim that in certain first-personal utterances, such as 'I am in ecstasy', the first person has no self-referential role, and the predicate no descriptive role; the utterance as a whole has merely ecstasy-behavioural 'status' on a par with a groan and a grimace. Wittgenstein allowed the first person self-referential work only in the apparently non-paradoxical cases where a material or body predicate is concerned. This exhibits the forced move that either our first-personal vocabulary will function on the apparently safe model of our *im*personal vocabulary, or, where certain first-personal utterances cannot be pressed into the impersonal mould, because, say, of their incorrigibility, they are lifted in the old positivistic fashion, entirely out of an assertive role and into a purely expressive one. Pressure puts Wittgenstein, like Ryle, on the side of the 'other' for the sake of coherence.

The paradoxes which motivate such re-location of certain first-person utterances are well known. These paradoxes derive from the apparent idiosyncrasy of certain first-person-related utterances. That is, what is present to the first person as he legitimately makes certain claims about himself seems unavailable to others as they make 'similar' claims about him and also unavailable to him when he makes 'such' claims about others.

This is the central point in much of the Philosophy of Mind, and it introduces the matters of Solipsism, Private Language, Other Minds, Persons and Things, and so on. The point that there is some such troublesome asymmetry seems to have been swallowed by most, if not all, philosophers writing in this area either as something to live with or to take conceptual or metaphysical action against. Strawson, for example, accepts it as a 'metaphysical' fact of the personal situation that some fundamental asymmetry exists between my P-claims about myself and my P-claims about others. Hence his view that although the meaning of what I say in these two cases is the same, the 'criteria' (what I feel 'in' myself and what I see, etc., of you) must differ. And hence his need for the concept of a Person to underwrite the saving identity of meaning and to close in metaphysical fashion the gap created by the acceptance of the dogma that I cannot in principle at *every* point say the self-same things about you as I can about me.

Consequently, I spend a good deal of time in Chapters VI and VII on questions of whether we can provide a relevant and useful sense to 'I know that you are in pain in just the way that I know I am in pain'. I believe we can so provide. Furthermore, there is so much at stake on this matter of the identity of our inter-personal states that no repair work as attempted by Strawson or avoidance tactics as attempted by Ryle or Place and Smart will work. No positions which have been first moved by the asymmetry between the relevant first-person and other-person cases can be correct positions. I hope to show there are not such troublesome asymmetries either between selves and others or between selves and things; nor does the final symmetry stem from a 'logical reduction' of one to the other. Such asymmetries as there actually are, turn out to be contingent upon irrelevant matters such as the economics of the interplay between context and convention and our contingent lack of ability to duplicate some inter-personal cases as readily as others. Hence, moves made to avoid the threat of paradox naturally would turn out to be otiose at best. There is no paradox to move against.

The denial that there are asymmetries which produce paradox does not, as I have said, mean the sequel seeks to identify, say, sensations as brain processes. That, too, is a view meant to avoid the apparent and usual difficulties of reconciling certain first-person ascriptions of sensations with second- or third-person ascriptions of sensations. On one view, this identification, probably at one time attributable to Place and Smart, avoids the real difficulty of how sensations and brain processes *are* related by denying that there are sensations *and* brain processes. There is the alternative and more reasonable interpretation, also attributable to Place and Smart, that sensations and brain processes, although not themselves identified, are nevertheless alternative descriptions of the identical event. They are, as J. J. C. Smart[1] puts it, '*as a matter of fact*' identical. What you feel is not, literally, what someone might see of you – i.e. certain of your brain processes – but, what someone might see of you may be used as a fully alternative description of and reference to what you feel. This interpretation of the Place and Smart position seems of little moment as against the sceptic, even though we may eventually find *some*thing like it to be true, since it merely re-institutes the original question put by

[1] See Chapter V, 'Consciousness', in Smart's *Philosophy and Scientific Realism*, 1963, which contains a later version, one presumes, than the 1959 *Philosophical Review* article, 'Sensations and Brain Processes'.

the asymmetrist or sceptic: how *do* we establish that to talk of brain processes is an alternative and independent way of referring to sensations? Views like this which seek to achieve a transfer of operations from predicates, such as 'sensation', which are troublesome in the first person, to a set of predicates, such as 'brain processes', which are paradigmatic of other person cases, are predictably unhappy as solutions to what troubles us about Other Minds. This is so, I shall argue, since to accept the need for such a transfer of operations is to accept an original asymmetry between first person and other person uses of certain predicates which itself is so far-reaching that *no* predicates survive it and thus nothing could work against it. Brain processes, I shall argue, are conceptually no more sceptic-proof than sensations; or sensations are conceptually as safe as brain processes. But the physicalists import brain processes as if they could so save the day from the sceptic.

Finally, we become involved in basic questions about the principles employed in the governance of 'same' and 'different'. We do, because it may turn out that 'A has the same sensation as B' will survive the sceptics' moves with the identical sturdiness of expressions such as 'A has the same brain state as B'. And hence, the reduction of sensations to brain states, or their 'identity in fact', would be postcedent to, although perhaps implied by, a solution to the Problems of Other Minds.

Abstract

This is an attempt to deal with a form of difficulty we have in reconciling recalcitrant aspects of our personal vocabulary. The difficulty seems to be centred in an apparent asymmetry between certain first-person and other-person expressions. Naturally other problems associated with this asymmetry are also of concern.

I. To begin with there seem to be *both* important similarities and differences between the things we are able to say of others and the things we may say of ourselves; but the differences apparently align themselves systematically; or so the sceptic might argue. This systematic asymmetry seems to follow the distinction between first-person and other-person uses of certain predicates. On the other hand there seem to be powerful arguments to the effect that such systematic differences, as between self-ascription and other-ascription, cannot be coherently countenanced. The first chapter attempts to weigh in an *a priori* fashion the viability of an asymmetry in our personal vocabulary. This approach will not, however, settle the matter. The fact that the first person *is* asymmetrical to the others seems to persist and balance those arguments which caution against its implications. A fuller account of the nature of this asymmetry and its importance to the personal paradoxes is required.

II. To satisfy this requirement the special asymmetrical features of the first person are discussed. These special features in contrast with the functions of the other personal pronouns seem to be required in order to state the personal paradoxes or to make a sceptical case. An attempt is then made to outline the role and test the necessity of the features unique to the first person.

III. But none of the special first-person features seems to be essential to the achievement of self-reference. This suggests that the personal sceptic or paradox-maker may have mistaken the role of these non-necessary but highly economical aspects of the first person. An attempt is made to show that without such a misconstruction of the role of the first person the sceptic cannot make his case. Our personal paradoxes seem to depend for their statement upon a special use of the first person or some such other asymmetrical device. But the trouble-making asymmetry of the first person is not indispensable to the function of self-reference. It may then be the case that our personal paradoxes give way just to the extent that we see the affinities between the first person and our other conventions of reference. A weaker thesis is made available for the faint of heart.

The second and third persons are discussed with an eye to illustrating the incoherence of taking the asymmetry of the first person as ineluctable since 'equally powerful asymmetries' are present at least in the second person and likely in the third person. Such a symmetrical asymmetry provides further reasons for taking all three persons as non-paradoxically interchangeable. Furthermore, it removes the two-fold contrast between selves and others needed and pressed for by the sceptic, replacing it with the *reductio* of a three-fold contrast between me, you and he.

IV. Private language is discussed from the point of view of the function of the first person convention. First, however, it must be argued that the interesting case of private language depends for its formulation upon the distinction apparently available within the first person. But the first person convention so overburdens the notion of private language that it now contains precisely what it hoped to extrude.

V. Epistemological questions naturally arise. Before they are directly handled some guide lines are set out by examining some of the implications of speech as action. Since *some* medium of interchange, successful or not, among persons is presupposed in the sceptic's case these implications may be important. It seems to turn out that crucial questions as to the point of speaking at all, the function of the hearer, the implied role of 'systematically ulterior motives', and so on, cannot begin to be answered on sceptical accounts which insist upon some form of epistemological asymmetry in principle.

VI. With the assurance that a systematic epistemological asymmetry is untenable we are free to look for other causes of difference between certain first-person claims and certain impersonal claims. The tendency of the argument is then to show that there are no special features to even the most troublesome of first-person claims which are not also exactly to be found among impersonal claims. The tendency of the argument is to show the lack of asymmetry between our personal and impersonal vocabulary.

VII. In parallel with this the traditional distinction between personal self-ascriptions (P_1-ascriptions) and material self-ascriptions (M_1-ascriptions) is examined and found wanting. In particular that purportedly distinguishing property of P-ascriptions which finds them 'shifting' in some sense or other between their first-person and other-person uses is examined. But no such 'shift', which is not also apparent in non-P cases, is found; we are not, for instance, limited, as is commonly thought, in our other-ascriptions of P-predicates merely to our observations of another's behaviour, or brain states, or any functional state of the organism. Finally an attempt is made to explain why we should have (mistakenly) thought that some of the things I might say of myself were to have been marked off from other things I might say of myself and from all of those things I might say of others.

I. The *A Priori* Deadlock

1. *Are pronoun differences or similarities to be dominant?*

An important matter in the philosophy of the Person is whether we are more impressed by the differences rather than the similarities between typical uses of the first personal pronoun on the one hand, and typical uses of the other personal pronouns on the other hand.

An impressive difference in their use has been that although all pronouns may be voiced by any particular speaker, 'I' occurs in his mouth unlike 'you' or 'he'. And since there is but a single list of epithets, which seem to connect to all pronouns without prejudice, the above difference will seem to introduce a double life into this list. Well-known sceptical problems ensue when such double life is granted the predicates of personal pronouns.

Ancillary differences, between 'I . . .' and, say, 'He . . .' locutions, would be in their manner of verification and, strangely, the absence of a noun which stands in relation to the first personal pronoun as do some nouns stand in relation to the other persons. There seems to be no noun or noun phrase of which the first personal pronoun could be pronominal – no such a noun as 'I' is a pronoun. 'I' may be used only by me of myself. No other substantive has that quality.

On the other hand there are persuasive similarities. 'I' may be used by any speaker, just as may 'you' or 'he'. Also, words which go with one of the personal pronouns and not with the others are difficult to come by, at least telling ones are. There is also the indefinite pronoun, 'one', which if truly indefinite and truly a pronoun would seem to blanket what is variable in personal pronouns. Moreover if 'we' is the honest plural of 'I' its close affinity to the plurals of the other pronouns reflects back upon the similarities of the singular forms of these pronouns. And of course the sceptical paradoxes which may accompany the accentuation of differences among these pronouns have been suasory in forcing the acceptance of their similarities as overriding. These things will concern us again.

Suppose for the moment we hold a neutral attitude toward the significance, and durability, of the differences and similarities between first person and other person ascriptions. Then if we regard these differences and similarities as alternatively dominant we are faced with four simple possibilities. (a) We may insist that others are like oneself (I-I); (b) that oneself is no different from others (you-you); (c) that oneself is different from others (I-You), and to complete the list of sheer possibilities, (d) the converse of the last possibility. More fully, we have the following.

(a) We may take 'I' and 'you' as basically similar expressions with 'I' as the overbearing so that self-ascription and other-ascription provide but a single life for their predicates but with the self serving as the paradigm of that life. We could dub this possibility 'I-I' and it would mean that 'your shame' may mean the same as 'my shame' as regards 'shame'; and 'my shame', not 'your shame', is to be the touchstone so that its differences or excesses, if any, are to be matched in 'your shame', while any differences or excesses in 'your shame' need not be matched in 'my shame'.

(b) Or we may take 'I . . .' and 'You . . .' still as locutions which do not create double lives for their predicates so that, say, 'shame' might still complete both locutions without ambiguity. But, unlike the first case, 'I . . .' is taken as a variant of 'You . . .', rather than *vice versa*, with a similar inversion in the matching of their similarities and differences. This case we might call 'You-You'.

(c) Or we might find 'I' and 'you' sufficiently different to maintain that difference and treat their ascriptions as seriously separate rather than as variants one of the other. In this case there is no attempt to hide a double life in our personal predicates or to force differences from either 'I' or 'you' onto the other. This possibility would be 'I-You'.

(d) And there is left its non-viable converse, 'You-I', which might however have interesting point-of-view consequences in fiction.

A further possible complication need only be limned at this point. If we assume that the 'criteria' for correct application of personal pronouns sometimes differ from another aspect of their use, say their 'meaning', then our list of possibilities is raised to sixteen. An interesting one, used by Strawson,[1] is as follows. Self-ascription and other-ascription take place by means of a common list of predicates. But their use in 'I . . .' locutions is to be the paragon of their use. This is the first case above, I-I. If we then introduce the possibility that the criteria for the correct application of these terms differ from their meaning, the situation becomes: 'You are sad' means the same as 'I am sad' as regards being sad but the criteria for correct application of the first sort of sentence differ from those for the second sort. In this case the apparent differences of 'I' from 'you' are forced upon 'you', as regards 'meaning', while the differences of 'you' are retained as second and third person criterial differences. The other fifteen possibilities are easily gathered but need not be since most things which need to be may be said within the four simpler divisions above.

2. *The argument from necessary plurals which seems to settle the issue*

Against the background of the set of possibilities offered by this scheme I should like to look at an argument which urges a particular reduction of the list of viable alternatives. It may be called the argument from necessary plurals and runs in its special application to the personal pronouns, as follows. When we speak of ourselves and use the first personal pronoun and its predicates it cannot be that others may not be univocally spoken of with these same predicates. For, if it were the case that others

[1] In the chapter on Persons in *Individuals*, Methuen, 1959.

may not be spoken of in the same way, then 'I' would be a systematically ambiguous expression as voiced by different speakers. How then would it do its work in even a single case? And it could not be retaliated, in the spirit of reform, that only I have a right to use 'I'. Such a point may not be argued unless you are here able to supply 'only' with a sensible function. But exceptives such as 'only' must be allowed possible plurality for their work.[1] Such unique urging, as a sceptic would require, would have to rest finally upon the possibility of an entity unique in principle – a difficult notion to muster.

3. *The argument from necessary plurals is indecisive as regards two possibilities*

If 'I' is not to be incoherent it must then be usable by others . . . usable by others as well as myself; the coherent use of 'I' calls into use the notion of others. And these others are the 'yous' and 'hes' of when I use 'I' of myself. Sometimes I myself am the 'you' and the 'he'. Given this freedom of interchange it is unlikely that our personal predicates will not be cashable at par among the various personal pronouns. 'I am ashamed' and 'you are ashamed' may be univocal as regards 'shame'. There are other ways of emphasizing the argument from necessary plurals. We might say as Strawson does in *Individuals* (p. 100) that anything which is mine cannot be mine could it only (logically) be mine. 'Mine' needs an equally rich contrast. Or we might say that any term capable of focusing our attention upon a particular particular must at least be capable of owning a plural, capable of being differentiated at some level from others of its own kind; we might say particulars must be open to fellowship.

Further, if 'we' is the honest plural of 'I' or, if 'I' has any legitimate plural, then 'you' and 'he', being the only candidates

[1] It might be worth having a closer look at exceptives such as 'only' as they function in support of a sceptic or solipsist. An article of mine, called 'Exceptives and Other Minds', in *Analysis*, 1959, attempts to do so.

for membership in that plurality are units of the same status. If on the other hand 'I' is incapable of being pluralized we are back again at absolute uniqueness and its incoherence. This all simmers down to the simple idea that 'I' and 'you' and 'he' mark a distinction in an interdependent fashion. They are of the same category.

If correct, this argument does reduce the number of live options in our list. It means that only the symmetrical options survive, that only those options will survive which offer personal predicates univocity. Of the four possibilities, I-I and You-You remain.

Strawson, for instance, believes that since 'you' and 'I' must both, on the strength of the above argument or its parallel, be served by a univocal list of predicates, the indicated option is I-I. This is, I think, a gratuitous assumption. The argument from necessary plurals points symmetrically to the You-You possibility. If we suppose that the use of one pronoun requires the apposite use of others, we have in accepting the fact of such dependence not yet decided its direction. All we have decided is that there do not seem to be certain forms of *in*dependence among the personal pronouns.

Granted that some of the aspects of these pronouns do not *prima facie* match up are we in accepting the argument, which nevertheless urges aspects of parity, then to see one or other of the pronoun sets as dominant in establishing this parity? Strawson supposes the differing 'I' aspects to be dominant. (Whatever 'you' differences there are are accommodated by having differing sets of criteria for the application of the 'same' predicates.) But there do not seem to be any immediate reasons for not accepting the possible dominance of the 'you' aspects. I want to examine this possibility in Chapter II but intend mainly to let it sort itself out since my arguments will anyway tend to show that we need not choose between the I-I and the You-You paradigms. They are parts of the same option. I want now rather to ask a question about the uniqueness of our personal demonstratives as a group, leaving open the question of whether there are relevant differences within the group. The question is whether our personal demonstratives may be supplanted in function by our impersonal demonstratives. I shall to begin with limit the argument to the first person case since it is the one most often defended as unique and since it also happily appears to be the most recalcitrant to impersonal reduction.

4. *An argument against the view that personal demonstratives are extrudable*

I want to begin this test of whether our personal demonstratives are eliminable by attempting to meet an important argument *against* the view that the use of personal subjects might constitute a particular form of linguistic feather-bedding.

In this historical argument, put forward most recently by Strawson in the third chapter of *Individuals*, 'Persons' are taken to be a set of particulars referred to by our personal pronouns and indispensable to the normal operations of our personal predicates. This personal subject, the notion of a Person, is held to be the basic subtending noun, or particular, presumed by the intelligible use of our personal vocabulary. Attempts to preempt the function of this personal subject by means of the offices of, say, impersonal subjects, meet with incoherence, it is argued. A perhaps crucial bit of evidence runs as follows.

Should you hold that personal pronouns do *not* perform a special introduction of a different sort of particular, your alternative is to see the apposition between a personal predicate and its personal pronoun as a mere verbal exchange for the actual relation between some, let's still say 'personal', predicate and some impersonal noun or noun phrase which in this case might be some discourse connected with complexly sensitive bodies. The attacking position claims that any attempt to formulate such a relation between an impersonal subject and a personal predicate would yield either circular or false claims or would still depend on some hidden personal subject. The attacking position here, we remember, would have it that only with a presumed type-distinct personal nominative is our personal discourse coherent.

In more detail the attack goes as follows. 'All my experiences are had by this body', is said to be the impersonal phrasing of the supposedly contingent relation between experiences and a particular body, while 'All my experiences are had by P', where 'P' stands for the personal particular, would be the non-reductionist rendering. The *im*personal advocate might attack this phrasing on the grounds that it amounts only to 'all my experiences are had by me', or 'all P's experiences are had by P' – unfruitful locutions in any case. The protagonist of Persons replies (*Individuals*, 97–98), that the relation between an experience and its owner must anyway be such that 'it is logically impossible that a particular state or experience is in fact possessed by someone else. The requirements of identity rule out the logical transferability of ownership'.

Moreover, the reductionist or impersonalist himself has not yet given an account of the residual personal pronoun 'my' in *his* own phrasing, 'All my experiences are had by this body'. He cannot simply drop this vestigial personal reminder since he would then be simply left with the falsity that all experiences are had by a particular body. He may, on the other hand, attempt to again shift the individuating work of *this* residual pronoun onto some impersonal noun phrase consistent with his reductionism.

But now, 'All my experiences are had by B', would seem to become, 'All B's experiences are had by B', or some form thereof, a statement no more fruitful than that criticized above, but still, no less defensible. If, as Strawson thinks, the personal pronoun is for reasons like these *in*extrudable in favour of impersonal terms then there would indeed seem to be room and need for another basic particular in expounding this area of ordinary discourse, and thus special irreducible work for our personal subjects.

But I think, with the issues still in their inchoate form, the personal pronoun may be eliminated without undue disturbance. Later as the issues change form we shall, I think, find the reasons and limitations connected with this elimination.

Let us be clear about one essential point disputed between an anti-reductionist of the role of personal demonstratives and his counterpart. Isn't it that one believes our personal pronouns to be pronominal of a *sui generis* personal particular while the other sees them at least as possible surrogates of impersonal particulars? But in both cases it is pronouns, surrogated or not, which may actually serve as subjects for or help offer introductions of or demonstrations with, personal predicates.

The disputed point would then be whether any impersonal term could help perform satisfactorily this introduction or demonstration or individuation normally accomplished with personal terms.

In any case, if the above setting of the problem is accurate it can only be a red herring to speak of experience being 'had' or not, 'possessed' or not, by a body or not. It is an accidental fact that the first personal pronoun possessive should be involved here anyhow; though it is true that adequate reference is often achieved by means of a possessive term. But the issue could probably be put with other forms of a personal subject. If it cannot, we may already be cashing in illicitly on a too-solitary sense of the first personal pronoun.

Obviously, the issue is also not just the question of the causal relations assertable of our personal predicates, though this again is often a valuable aid for identification. It is more likely that this is a question of a dependent order since such relations would be fruitful for us only after we had established the adequacy of an impersonal exchange for the personal subject. In other words, *adequately* to introduce our causal notions here is to beg the question against the personalist. What is first of concern then is whether an impersonal term may adequately help do the job of individuating experiences in the normal spatio-temporal or ostensive manner, in concert with a personal predicate. If we should come upon such a thing it will be something like a rule of reference and rules of reference are not, once we accept them as rules, contingent.

'All my experiences are had by my body'. This is, as it stands, only opaquely a proposition about whether bodies are or are not the particulars by means of which we are helped to identify an experience. We might ask, 'Is it *my* body?' If this has an answer, then here is a sense of 'my' extrudable in favour of, say, space-time reports. If it is not so extrudable then we are again on the road to solipsism since 'my' is left with a too-personal ring to it.

The next move in the attempted translation is then away from the unnecessary possessive idiom and to, 'All my experiences are had by *this* body.' Suppose we remove the causal redolence. 'All my experiences are identifiable with reference to this body'. And here we must again avoid the over-unique sense of 'my'. We do not want to cash in on a sense of 'my' which is systematically exclusive. Such a move would cash too well. It is difficult anyhow to see what the objection could be to the addition of another personal pronoun, for that is all that caution here would amount to. So we add an insert: 'All my experiences, *as well as those of others*, are identifiable with reference to bodies.' And *now* the duty of the expression, 'all my experiences as well as those of others' can be filled as well by the phrase 'all experiences'. Thus we get, 'All experiences are identifiable by reference to bodies', a seemingly articulate locution which has nevertheless extruded a personal pronoun by shifting its referential work to an impersonal term. More particularly, we could get the locution, 'This experience is identifiable with reference to this body' to stand in for 'My experience is had by this body.'

The fact that the substitution of impersonal for personal means of identification does not seem to resist articulation suggests that our personal pronouns are not terms which identify particulars of a *sui generis* sort. I intend to argue this in much more detail in the next chapter. But I want now to examine the way in which the postulation of a 'personal basic particular' might have been thought to have helped the situation. It *should* come out, on the strength of what has just passed, that such a postulation would not have been of help.

5. *Does a personal particular help?*

In the ingenious chapter on Persons in his book *Individuals*, there occurs a statement of late but central importance to Strawsons' kind of position against certain aspects of scepticism. This statement is to the effect that though the meaning of a certain class of so-called personal predicates must, *a priori*, be the same in cases of both self- and other-ascription the criteria of such ascription may differ in each case. The coherence of all this is underwritten by the function of the notion of a Person. I want to argue that Strawson's use of the notion of Person is ineffective against the sceptic and leaves the position precisely where it was before Persons were introduced as a conceptual aid against the sceptic. Before I try to show this I want first to clear away as unhelpful a criticism which has been made against Strawson's criteria-meaning split.[1]

The issue is this. Strawson claims there is a difference in the criteria but not in the meaning of a personal predicate according as the predicate is involved within a first personal pronoun context or within a second and third personal pronoun context; and these two sets of criteria, though different, are each logically adequate to do, as it were, not different work.

To argue within Strawson's terms, suppose for the moment we accept the difference here between 'meaning and criteria'. Strawson says, we 'ascribe personal predicates to others on the strength of observation of their behaviour; and (these) behaviour criteria one goes on are not just the signs of the presence of what is meant by the P-predicate, but are criteria of a logically adequate kind for the ascription of the P-predicate (106)'. We ascribe personal predicates to ourselves on other grounds,

[1] See 'Pains, Puns, Persons and Pronouns', by Freed and Foder, *Analysis*, 1961.

whatever they are. But in both cases, mine and yours, these predicates *mean the same*. 'It is not that these predicates have two kinds of meaning. Rather it is essential to the single kind of meaning that they do have, that both ways of ascribing them should be perfectly in order (110)'.

It could be argued against this business of a criterial difference in self- and other-ascription of personal predicates, that it merely reinstates a systematically ambiguous reading of P-predicates and that there must then be a 'uniform set of conditions' or the same criteria associated with both self- and other-ascription to avoid this slide-back. 'He is in pain', like 'I am in pain', it might be claimed, is associated with, let us say, having an unpleasant feeling.

One might be reinforced in this conclusion by the clue that whatever Strawson is to mean by 'criteria' his thesis of a criterial difference for personal dicta will not go through. Strawson's position was that in order to have two independent sets of criteria operable, then, *sometimes* (99) at least, the less favoured criteria, the behavioural ones, must be logically adequate.[1] This might incur the obvious objection that Smith may be in pain under *any* conditions of his overt behaviour, and contrariwise, that no complaint of Smith's could guarantee that he is suffering. Thus it would seem behaviour criteria cannot be logically adequate for the ascription of personal predicates to others.

But this move incurs the more obvious counter-objection that Smith couldn't be in pain under *any* systematically varying conditions of his overt behaviour, nor, contrariwise, could *no* complaint of his ever 'guarantee' that he is suffering. These sorts of measures are just what we have to make our peace with in cases of other-ascription. I hope, however, to show in Chapter VII that the basis of our trust in such measures for other-ascription rests on precisely the same basis as do our measures for self-ascription.

[1] If we construe Strawson as offering a weaker role than 'logical adequacy' to other-ascriptive criteria the anti-sceptical weld he wants between selves and others is broken.

But, clearly, banking on an 'unpleasant feeling' as the 'uniform condition' associated with Smith's pain and my pain is just a way of fully re-introducing the original problem of how 'your unpleasant feeling' and 'my unpleasant feeling' are to be construed.

This point of a single kind of personal meaning and two ways of ascribing it has probably troubled most readers of *Individuals*. But I don't think its full unhappiness can be made out unless we bring in briefly the hoped-for function of the notion of a Person.

Adopting the concept of a Person as a basic particular is calculated to lend coherence to our personal vocabulary. If we presuppose such a basic underpinning then we have the underriding assurance that the differences between say, the uses of the first and other personal pronouns are only differences within a greater similarity. The sceptic is not given room to begin his prising.

But this is only a facade, for if we accept the differences between selves and others, at least as data to be reckoned with, then these differences will not so easily be covered in the way the notion of a Person seems to promise. These differences seem to be reconciled in Strawson's principle that though our personal predicates mean the same in self- and other-ascription (the result of assuming a common underpinning), the criteria of application of these predicates differ in the two cases (the result of still accepting the differences between selves and others). The split just reappears in another place, I want to argue, and re-introduces the problem the notion of Persons was meant to solve. And this reintroduction is, I think, systematic.

Suppose we accept the thesis that the intelligible use of our personal vocabulary indicates the underriding presence of the concept of a Person. Then our personal vocabulary ostensibly has the unity that is proof against scepticism. Whatever is said of me may univocally be said of you for it is a presupposition now that selves and others are both Persons, both of that whole cloth.

But there is, just mentionably, a different way of telling whether something is the case about you as opposed to when I say it is so of myself. The criteria differ but the meaning of what we ascribe to Persons, both ourselves and others, is the same.

What is this communal inter-personal meaning of a particular personal remark to be? It must come, as it were, from the self for we do not need the underwriting provided by the notion of Persons to allow us to say of ourselves what we can say of *others*. It is the converse case which needs coherence. Suppose then, when you are said to be anxious, that it means the same as when you yourself say you are anxious; no split between 'me' and 'you'. The criteria, if such they are, used in saying this of you, are of course public criteria. But what will be the conditions for you correctly to say this of yourself? Suppose it is how you 'feel', or some other aspect of what the notion of Persons underwrites as nonsceptically sayable of both you and me. But if this is allowed then what is said of you will only be part of what is on other occasions ascribed to me – the rest will be reserved as criteria of self-ascription.

Now we are each provided with two *sets* of criteria, one for when we want to say correctly, each of himself, that we are anxious, another for when we want to say this of another. And now the notion of a Person must assure me not only that I mean the same as do you when either of us says something of himself; and not only that we mean the same when we say something of others as we mean when we say it of ourselves (and thus that the behaviour criteria we use in saying things of others will sometimes be logically adequate); *but it must also assure us that my criteria are the same as yours when each of us says something of himself.* But the concept of a Person is unable, I think, except by highly gratuitous fiat, to gurantee such community of self-ascriptive criteria since it has already allowed a difference of criteria between the cases of self- and other-ascription despite the same community of meaning there desired. The concept of a Person legislates similarity only for meaning and not for criteria. That is how it bridges the sceptic's gap.

To argue that criteria or conditions are to be the same where what they rule over (i.e. meaning) is the same could only be successful, I think, in both cases or in neither case. Nor, for that matter, can it be argued that my criteria for saying something of myself may be different than yours for yourself. The concept of a Person does not require that our criteria be different; it permits a one-many relation between the meaning of what we say and the criteria employed. Such permissiveness leaves it arguable then whether the criteria in question are similar *or* different. But arguable somehow it must be or we then merely re-issue the sceptic's licence in another only faintly removed locale: Are my criteria for saying something of myself anything like your criteria for saying that same thing of yourself?

Another possibility seems to remain. We might claim there are criteria only in the case of other-ascription while self-ascription requires none. But then we should have a split of another sort than among criteria. It would be a difference now in the form of 'I...' locutions from 'you...' locutions as pressed by the proposed absence of conditions of correctness in the former case. This has been called the 'no ownership' theory; but its acceptance just firms up the asymmetry between 'no ownership' uses of the first person and the absence of such cases in the other persons. It is probably essential anyhow to argue for a common function among personal locutions, i.e. something like 'ascription', or something like a referring role for 'I', in order to find use for the theory of Persons as basic particulars. The notion of a Person has use only as a means of reducing just such asymmetries. Isn't it precisely the agglomerated difficulty of achieving community of form among personal utterances which conscripts the concept of a Person to its aid? Difference of form seems then an unlikely alternative as far as the defence of the concept of a Person is concerned. Hence if self-ascription is, even in some of its cases, said to be non-criterially achieved surely it would be a much stronger tool than is mere difference of criteria with which to dismantle the univocity of interpersonal meaning proposed by the introduction of the concept of a Person.

In other words, isn't the sceptic in precisely the same position of strength as before the notion of a Person was introduced to foil him?

6. *Some arguments for and against personal uniqueness*

It could still be objected that any attempted pre-emption of a basic role for personal demonstratives is not crucial or complete for it was performed only with the bracketing of the most powerful of personal factors, those private aspects of the self which seem to offer independence of the identificatory locus provided by one's body. We need then to look back at the first of the propositions of fruit for the sceptic. That was the proposition of the uniqueness of some aspects of the self.

When he is tending the fire, it is claimed there are certain aspects of that situation which might be different to him than to anyone else though he might not speak of them differently than might anyone else. One might then say that 'his tending the fire' or 'my tending the fire' are expressions which cannot retain this sense of, consciousness shall we say, if their inherent pronouns are completely evacuated in favour of impersonal terms, since these personal terms are meant precisely to capture those uniquely personal aspects from among the impersonal.

Perhaps these unique aspects of the self, these private aspects, might have their status as special idio-items tested by again trying just such a substitution as is contra-indicated by their nature, that is by seeing whether impersonal terms may capture that personal uniqueness.

Suppose we take 'My states of consciousness cannot be the states of consciousness of anyone else', or 'My x is non-transferably owned', as indicative of the sense of the uniquely personal aspects. 'States of consciousness', or, 'x', would be variables for any 'non-material' predicate expression which might normally follow a personal subject. (How we draw the line for personal predicates need not now be at stake.)

The important thing about this uniquely personal aspect is its touted non-applicability or non-transferability to any other subject: a hint of Leibnitz. We remember, parenthetically, that the problem of the status of similarities within such highly personal terms, the problem of how there may be personal predicates where such uniqueness *is* touted, is just the problem of the sceptical split in our personal vocabulary.

It may then be worth examining this business of non-transferability away from its personal ramifications for the moment, and in a place where we may be somewhat clearer. That is, we might examine non-transferability among impersonal locutions with an eye to whether its character there will allow its competent substitution back into the personal idiom; and if not, why not.

We look then for an ascription to a particular physical object which is non-transferable to other objects. Given normal predicates and the argument from necessary plurals we may say out of hand that all of them will be other-ascribable rather than non-transferable. 'But', you might argue, 'the particular colour, say of this hand, is the colour which only this hand may have. Its colour is *its* colour. That it may be duplicated or have kindred exemplifications is beside the point'. What *would*, however, constitute an example of the non-transferable uniqueness in question, would be the other-ascription of an already particularized property.

When we see that an example would require the other-ascription of an already particularized property it is clearer, I think, why our ordinary predicates cannot play this tune.

If they could we should have to forego our rules of individuation or particularization. For it is an already particular exemplification we are being asked to other-ascribe. Here then is what we cannot other-ascribe from one impersonal object to another, we cannot other-ascribe an object's systematically individuating features. We cannot for instance other-ascribe its space-time history. But it is probably mistaken to feel that any of the object's properties are systematically unique or individual in the way its space-time history may be. Imagine, for example, pressing the point of the uniqueness of a particular case of yellow without the use of a demonstrative. Or imagine drawing the conclusion that each different subject requires its own non-transferable string of predicates. Imagine concluding to a solipsism of object, as it were. It is the case, rather, that this particular ascription of yellow is induplicable, if it is, because of its individuating ties; and these individuating ties will have nothing to do with yellow, if one is forced to speak this way, but will emerge when we have unpacked the demonstrative. That is the aspect of its history which may not be other-ascribed. If there is a sense to the absolutely unique it is contained in our rules of individuation of impersonal objects.

Suppose we try to work this business back upon those personal non-transferable aspects. Here we shall need a demonstrative-like term, in this case 'my', to press the 'special' uniqueness of this or that state. My fever cannot be ascribed to or be had by anyone else in the way it is had by or ascribed to me. (Compare: This colour cannot be ascribed to or had by anything else in the way it is had by or ascribed to this hand.)

Perhaps this personal demonstrative marks a personal particular in connection with which the fever is individuated. I have tried to show that at least one objection in principle against the take-over of our personal demonstratives by our impersonal ones does not hold. In the next chapter I shall ask in more detail whether or not our personal demonstratives perform an indispensable task. But we may waive this kind of consideration for the moment and ask independently whether our impersonal demonstratives can engender the required aspect of uniqueness our personal demonstratives seem capable of.

And of course our impersonal demonstratives are in this regard just as capable: 'This fever cannot be ascribed to or had by anything else in the way it is ascribed to or had by this body'.

If one insists upon asking whether the distinction between personal uniqueness and impersonal uniqueness is retained when personal demonstratives are dropped, if one insists upon asking if 'that fever' or 'the fever which so-and-so' can retain the sense of 'his fever', the reply is that 'his' is not a rich enough demonstrative to do its work in exile from our usual impersonal individuating patterns. It is probably misleading to ask if two different kinds of uniqueness, one personal and one impersonal, have occurred *at all*, since it is actually a question of whether two different kinds of individuation, one personal and one impersonal, are possible. And the trouble with 'personal' individuation is that it stops only at solipsism.

This particular defence of the unique aspects of the self which, in this form and others to be looked at, creates most of the difficulties in our personal idiom may then be seen at this early point in the development of the argument as a kind of Leibnitzian illusion, the illusion that because individuals are systematically unique their properties are too. It is probably best to say that neither or only both together are unique. This, as everyone knows, is to think of subject-and-predicate as an indisoluble tool with the accidental but economical virtue of having repeatable terms attachable to differently headed sentences.[1] We might introduce a convention where our demonstratives (i.e. uniqueness), are built more closely into our predicates, for apparently to have them as far away as the subject is to tempt the forgetful. With such a thought in mind it becomes difficult even to raise the point of the preter-uniqueness of some personal or even impersonal properties. We ask such questions only when we are not mindful enough of the unity of our demonstrative and descriptive conventions as they work together in a particular case. But there are not two such types of question we cannot ask unless there are two types of demonstratives. All that the admission amounts to anyhow that our concept of the personal is collapsible into our concept of

[1] See S. Coval's 'Demonstrative without Descriptive Conventions' in *Philosophy*, October 1965.

the impersonal is just the admission that we have, as of now, only one kind of demonstrative and not two.

7. *The present state of the argument*

I want now to move on to more detailed arguments regarding the role of our personal pronouns. It is there the issue of selves *versus* others, and personal *versus* impersonal, will be largely settled; although this too will have to be argued.

What I take the present state of the argument to be is as follows. There is a deadlock at the *a priori* level between accepting that selves must be like others and accepting that selves must essentially differ in some ways from others. The argument from necessary plurals and the uniqueness of the first person are the background opponents in this deadlock. The argument from necessary plurals seems incontrovertible and so, if the argument is not completely mis-stated, ground will have to be given by the view that the first person is a troublesomely unique demonstrative. This I shall pursue in the next section along with a lesser analysis of the other two persons.

Subsidiary arguments have shown in what ways the uniqueness of the first person or of the self-ascription of certain properties may *not* be made out. It will be of no help to the personal paradoxes, I have argued, to posit a basic personal particular. Nor may we defend the position in the ways in which it has been defended most recently, that our personal demonstratives are inextrudible in favour of impersonal ones. Lastly the ostensibly type-distinct personal factor of the uniqueness or non-transferability of some personal properties seemed explicable on other than *sui generis* grounds. We could produce non-transferability, in what seemed the only relevant sense, equally among impersonal objects. When we did so the notion of such non-transferable uniqueness was seen to be the idea of particularized properties and thus left behind only the issue of whether there are two different sorts of identification in use. The issue was not what it appeared to be before, namely of whether there is necessarily another mode of identification because some properties – certain personal ones – were in principle non-transferable. Non-transferability is a feature of *any* particularized predicate whatever its purported status.

I have indicated in which way I take the argument to this point to be leaning. But nothing has yet been produced which explains away the unique function of the first personal pronoun. And until this is done the argument, I think, cannot be moved far enough away from the sceptic's bias.

II. Personal Pronouns (A)

8. *Four things pursued*

It seems to me there exist some *bona fide* asymmetric features of our self-referential speech devices, which may themselves be related to the troublesome asymmetry between self-ascriptions and other-ascriptions: related, that is, to Scepticism about Persons. I want to show, however, that these asymmetric features of the first person are due to our convened capitalization, with great economic results, upon certain interesting aspects of the speech situation. Hence, these asymmetric features of our first-personal device, I hope to show, are not sufficient to mark a systematic distinction; and if they are not so sufficient it will be at least more difficult to argue that first-person ascriptions differ in some systematic way from other-person ascriptions. *That* argument would seem to require that the asymmetries of our self-referential devices with respect to our other demonstratives be more than a matter of economic contingency.[1]

I hope then to do the following. 1. To set down the special features of the first person, our (main) device of self-reference. 2. To test which of these special features we could replace and yet still achieve successful self-reference. 3. To offer an account

[1] It is partly because Strawson, for instance, finds that self-reference cannot be accomplished successfully by impersonal demonstratives that he moves toward the position of Persons as 'basic particulars'. See pp. 94–98 in *Individuals*. There is also Wittgenstein's view as reported by G. E. Moore in *Mind*, January 1955, p. 14, that a first-personal utterance like 'I am in pain' does not embody referential uses of the first person at all but is rather merely an aspect of pain behaviour itself. *Both* Strawson and Wittgenstein find our personal demonstratives troublesomely asymmetric with respect to our impersonal ones.

of the importance of the special features of the first person, of why we retain those particular first-person features which turn out to be non-necessary. 4. In Chapter IV I hope to see how the Personal Sceptic is affected by the fact that certain key features of our device of self-reference turn out to be non-necessary. Perhaps his scepticism about persons will turn out to be non-necessary in the same way.

9. *Special features of the first person*

I take the following features of the first person, taken together, to be shared by no other demonstrative.

(a) Only I may use 'I'[1] of myself.
(b) Anyone may use 'I' of himself.
(c) Only the speaker may use 'I' (only) of himself.

The first two features of the first person taken together allow us a parallel with one of the Sceptic's main ambivalences about Persons. Compare, 'Only I may say "I" of myself, yet still anyone may say "I" of himself', with, 'Only I may in a sense ascribe certain aspects of my personal states (P-states), to myself and yet, anyone may ascribe his P-states to himself'.

Both of these contrasting couples interestingly seem to produce the same form of rub: (i) Does 'I' mean the same when others use it of themselves as when I use it of myself? Or, when they say 'you' or 'he' of me do they mean what I mean when I say 'I' of myself? After all, only *I* may say I of myself. (ii) Does my self-ascription mean the same or have the same criteria as do the self-ascriptions of others? Or when others ascribe certain P-states to me do they mean the same as I do when I ascribe such states to myself? After all, only *I* may self-ascribe certain aspects of my P-states to myself. Etc.

I don't here care to argue what everyone will agree to – that such forms of Scepticism about Persons lead to certain in-

[1] I may of course use ' "I" ' of another in reporting or reproducing his speech about himself.

coherences. I intend rather to try to undermine such forms of argument by providing an account of one distinction crucial to at least some sceptical approaches such that this distinction is rendered useless and indeed hostile to sceptics about Persons. The distinction in question is that between the function of the first person and the function of our other demonstratives.

10. *Are the special features of the first person needed for the performance of self-reference?*

I want now to see whether the special features of our first person device are specially required for the achievement of self-reference or whether unique self-reference may be achieved without them. I shall examine three candidates for substitution of the device of the first person. Each of these candidates I think would achieve for us unique self-reference but none of them has all the properties of the first person. We shall then want to ask what if anything is served by those special properties of the first person.

We might introduce a convention of speaker-restricted 'names'. In such a case there are 'names' which each of us uses only of himself. What backs up the success of such a rule is a set of particular conventions governing the use of each speaker-restricted name so that we may know it *is* speaker-restricted in its application. There will have to be such individual conventions because there is, *ex hypothesi*, no formally general way of indicating the difference between such speaker-restricted and non-speaker-restricted 'names'. But, this device of separate speaker-restricted 'names', though it could supply us with unique self-reference, loses the economy and generality of our first person device – that anyone may use 'I' of himself. It does not satisfy characteristic (b). I shall expand this soon.

Instead of a convention of speaker-restricted 'names' we could use our proper names as they are now used; but to distinguish cases where we want unique *self*-reference we would add an *ad hoc* convention such as pointing to oneself. This too would get us unique self-reference. Also it seems more economical than the previous suggestion since we do not now need two sets of names, one speaker-restricted and one other-restricted, plus a host of individual conventions to convey the speaker-restrictedness of these 'first-person names'. In using what are normally other-restricted names all we need add is something like the use of the general convention of pointing to oneself as one utters one's name.

Of course the trouble with the use of normal proper names as a means of self-reference is that they are normally used to refer to others. When we do use them of ourselves they are usually so usable only *via* their connection with a form of the first person. But if our normal practice were to use them both for self-reference and other-reference we should be prepared for this possible but clearable ambiguity rather than accepting as necessary what was merely normal practice. The difference between using normal proper names plus pointing as against specially restricted 'names' for self-reference is that in the first case, but not in the second, we must keep reciting the rule, i.e. pointing, which associates the name with the individual ('this is Enos') whenever there is doubt about which individual is referred to. But there aren't two kinds of doubt, as it were: doubt about whether you are other-referring or self-referring; these are the same order of doubt, namely, who is being talked about? On the other hand, in the case of a set of 'names' specially restricted to self-referential use what we have is the same kind of rule of association governing the special set of names as governs the set restricted normally to other-reference: there is no difference of kind between Enos' introduction of himself as 'Enos is the man before you', and your introduction of him as 'Enos is the man before you'. The rule, or description, or association which relates this unique name uniquely to him will be of the same sort which would relate to him the name which *we* use of him and which with other associative rules he might conceivably use of himself.

Other candidates of substitution for the first person, such as special predicate inflections or the use of the general demonstrative 'this', rather than particular demonstratives such as names, are unimportantly different from the cases already scouted. To inflect our predicates so that the first, the second, and the third person distinction is retained is only the most trivial of changes from our established use of personal pronouns, amounting to the difference between 'I see' and something like 'see I'; or the difference between 'I am cold' and 'Am cold'.

The use of 'this' as a surrogate for 'I' differs from the use of a self-restricted proper 'name' in that while 'this' satisfies the characteristic of generality that anyone may use 'this', it does not satisfy the restrictive feature that only the speaker, or only I, may use 'this' of myself. In this respect it is no different than the use of ordinary proper names for self-reference since, like names, 'this' would with appropriate changes be usable by anyone of himself but would not be uniquely restricted to use by the speaker of himself. But the situation in which a term, like 'this' may be used to identify does not differ relevantly from the situation in which 'Enos' may be used to do so.

The point of these cases is merely to show that though these surrogates may fail to fit some of the characteristics of our particular self-referring device of the first person they are yet each adequate to perform the function, if not to duplicate what I shall argue is the economy, of that device. This would suggest that the characteristics not shared by these surrogate ways of performing the function are not essential to that function.

II. *Are the personal pronouns essential to the formulation of the paradoxes?*

I want to leave the above topic for the time being and turn to another of the related topics in this section: in what sense are our personal pronouns, as they stand, involved in the formulation of the personal paradoxes? At this point I do not wish to ask whether such formulations are themselves justified but only whether our attention to the personal pronouns at this stage is justified. A possible objection to their relevance would be that personal pronouns are contingent secondary aspects of our language and that it is possible to reconstruct the problems of persons independently of the use of such pronouns. Not much would change, it could be argued, were we to by-pass the personal pronouns and state our difficulties in terms of the other demonstratives available to us. And we have already seen that the distinction or function of at least the first person is duplicable by our other demonstratives.

But it is obviously unlikely that our difficulties with persons could be stated without at least the distinction between self-reference and other-reference and this is a distinction afforded within the personal pronouns even though it may be otherwise accomplished. And, because there are certain *other* special features to these pronouns, we had better stay with them on the chance that these other features contribute to the paradoxes though they are irrelevant for self-reference.

Another perhaps more venerable and associated way of arguing that the problems of persons do not lean on the speaker-hearer distinction or the distinction between speaker-restricted and other-restricted terms is to suggest we could begin a full reconstruction of these problems from one 'self' alone. But this is to suggest that an account of a speaker *qua* speaker could begin without involving its obvious contrasts; or it is to suggest that the first personal pronoun, our sole speaker-restricted term, has a function which does not tie it to the speaker-hearer situation but to a more primitive, let us say subjective situation; there could, however, as I have argued earlier, be in principle no general rule introduced for the use of 'I', no rule which would allow 'anyone to use "I" of himself', were it to be *first* over-restricted in the fashion such a view requires. Rather too lonely implications follow the systematic rejection of a general rule for the use of 'I'. The first person must necessarily have the generality which allows anyone to use it; and as I shall argue in Chapters V and VI, this must be so for some of the same reasons that our tools of other-reference must have a generality which indifferently allows anyone to use them.

To suggest that the first personal pronoun could function on its own and only later, contingently, become involved with the other personal pronouns, that self-reference precedes other-reference, is to work, I think, from a mistaken order of priorities. For instance, we shall shortly see in section 18 that 'I' has no asymmetries to its use which may not be countered by asymmetries unique to the second person, and has thus no leverage for its claim to priority.

Another objection to the focus of attention upon the personal pronouns as providing a key to the personal paradoxes is the supposition that 'think', 'feel', 'hope', 'try', 'understand', 'intend', 'act' are the sorts of terms crucial to the matter. It is not what we say these things *of*, but what we say *of* these things that is problematic, it is said.[1]

I do not care to deny that our psychological or personal predicates, their implications and use, are a source of the trouble we have in getting straight about Persons. There is an epistemological side to our difficulties with Persons. I try to address myself to it in Chapters V and VI. Here I am concerned to argue that there is a subject side, as well as predicate side, to the matter of our trouble with Persons: and that the subject side is a necessary condition of such trouble. Certain Phenomenologist and Existentialist uses of our first personal pronoun obliquely attest to this. The case of the Systematically Elusive I, dealt with in section 14, would be a case in point; and so would be Spiegelberg's comment on his own paper to the Western Division A.P.A., 1963, that 'I am me' is a seminal utterance for phenomenological analysis of the Self. The strong view that we cannot formulate the sceptic's desired asymmetry without some demonstrative distinction as we have *within* the personal pronouns is argued primarily in the next chapter.

It is worth noticing immediately, although superficially, that

[1] This is an objection raised by G. J. Warnock in criticism of an earlier version of this point – at least, this is what I took his objection to be.

were it the case that the action of our personal predicates *wholly* created the issues regarding Persons, we would be within our rights to expect the existence of many separate kinds of paradox such as the Paradox of Feeling, or the Paradox of Hoping, or the Paradox of Trying. But these are, as a matter of fact, not separate issues nor separate problems, at least with respect to Persons. Each is structurally identical with the rest as regards the personal paradoxes. It is not the many kinds of different things we say about persons which give us difficulty, rather it is the limited things common to much of what we say about persons which trouble us. We can thus expect a unified influence over the range of personal predicates which fits them to the personal paradoxes. A main influence or similarity is not, I think, far to seek.

For example, there is the issue ostensibly raised by the question of whether there is a double or single sense to our personal predicates as they are used self-ascriptively and other-ascriptively. It appears there are certain aspects or uses of the personal predicates which, suspiciously following the pronoun distinction, are either speaker-restricted or not. How a speaker-restricted or self-referential ascription may be articulate at all and how it may relate to non-speaker-restricted-ascription is surely a central problem for Persons. But it seems to me that none of this could begin to be problematic without the binding, trouble-making involvement of the very distinction afforded by the personal pronouns – the distinction between speaker and others or between self-reference and other-reference. *And this distinction is not a distinction of predicates*, personal or otherwise.

There is a more direct way of seeing how our personal predicates depend upon the personal pronouns for at least part of their problematic nature. Given our present conventions we might say that the so-called group of personal predicates must function in coupling with some demonstrative or introductory term. But for these predicates to function as purported they must be restrictable in the manner specially characteristic of the Personal idiom. A normal demonstrative such as 'this' or 'this body . . .' would not provide the restriction required to produce a personal paradox unless we tacitly tacked on to such demonstratives an additional notice of restrictive effect. Such a demonstrative as 'this' may be used by anyone but until special conventions have been understood it may not be used by anyone *of himself* alone. But granted that this could be arranged 'this' would now play a double role, restricted and non-restricted in its reference to the speaker. Without the additional restrictive notice, the new demonstrative will neither do its new self-referential job nor create the purported paradoxes which consist in the rub between self- and other-reference. There is no possibility of persuasively stating these paradoxes without cashing in on the presence of speaker-restricted versus non-speaker-restricted devices such as 'I' and 'you'.[1] And, we remember, it would not do as a real alternative to inflect speaker restriction directly into certain predicates since this would mean a hardly different way of providing for the distinction already carried by the personal pronouns.

It is this speaker-restricted or self-referential aspect of some *predicates* that gives this group the unity of the name 'personal'. And it is their dual service in *both* speaker-restricted and non-speaker-restricted contexts which is at least in part to blame for the emergence of the personal paradoxes.

But when you have said that some predicates are in some cases speaker-restricted and in some not, you have said not more than that some of them are introduced by the first personal pronoun and some not. And it is the consequence and necessity of *that* convention which need examination.

There is another form to this same objection against the relevance of the personal pronouns to the personal paradoxes.[2] It might be argued that there is no essential difference between a sentence of the form 'personal pronoun + personal predicate', and one of the form, 'impersonal demonstrative + personal preidcate'. Compare: (of a child) 'He is approaching now' and 'It's

[1] This is argued in section 16.

[2] Also raised, I believe, by Warnock.

approaching now'. We find, as well, little difference, it could be added, between utterances of the form, 'personal demonstrative + impersonal predicate' and those of the form, 'impersonal demonstrative + impersonal predicate'. Compare: (of a ship) 'She's sinking' with 'It's sinking'. In each set of examples the demonstratives are varied while the predicate is kept constant. The implication is, of course, that the nature of the demonstrative is irrelevant to our difficulties in reconciling two sets of predicates or two kinds of ascription.

A symptomatic weakness of this view is exposed if we allow the permissiveness shown in it toward our personal demonstratives to be turned upon the personal predicates. Compare: (of a ship) 'It's tired' with 'It's old, slow, and dilapidated'. We cannot plead trope here without allowing the same pleas in the demonstrative case. And were such permissiveness systematically possible in both cases there would be no trouble to the distinction between speaker- versus non-speaker-restricted utterances and thus no basis for any sort of type distinction between persons and things or between two kinds of ascription. And thus there would hardly be any basis for the personal paradoxes. This is an inconsistent position for what is put forward as an *alternative* way of *stating* these troublesome issues, i.e. in predicate terms alone.

In this section I tried to show something of the relation of the speaker-hearer distinction to the difficulties we seem to have with the apparently schismatic use of certain predicates. Any particular fashion of invoking the speaker-hearer distinction is, I argued, probably duplicable; but the personal pronouns in particular deserve our full attention since it is around this particular way of providing the distinction that the personal paradoxes actually and perhaps necessarily centre.

I want to proceed now to the third point of this chapter; that is to try to account for the nature and importance of those three uniquely united characteristics of the first person. Part of the point of this will be to keep separately before us which aspects of the first person are essential to its function as a device of self-reference and which not. Another part of the point will be whether these non-necessary aspects of the first person, which are likely to have an economic basis, perhaps are involved with the form of our personal paradoxes. It remains to be seen whether the personal paradoxes can or cannot be stated in the absence of the economics of the first person device as it stands. Should they be incapable of statement in the absence only of the economic aspects of the function of the first person then their solution might reside in that demonstration. After discussing these special features I hope it will be clear that they are not special enough problematically to contrast selves with others. I discuss the implications of this in section 16.

12. *The functions and importance of the special features of the first person*

I hope to begin to examine the special features of the first person by heuristically invoking some arguments for and against the inextrudability of the personal pronouns. Suppose the case of attempted substitution for the first person which we have just examined are successful cases. It may then be clearer what is actually at stake between those who would on the one hand find the function of our personal pronouns dispensable in favour of the operation of impersonal demonstratives as opposed to those who would on the other hand find *in*dispensable the use of some type-distinct speaker demonstrative.

We remember, for instance, that Strawson argues (see section 5, 'Does a Personal Particular Help?') in favour of a type-distinct personal demonstrative by claiming that formulations which tried to extrude them were bound to turn out either plainly false or tautologous. This is, I believe, a point which does have a good deal to it. The issue between those who do and those who do not find dispensable our personal indices would benefit, I think, from the separation of two of its aspects.

The first is the, I hope, now-clearer question of whether the function of our present speaker-restricted or self-referential device can or cannot merely be duplicated by a device which is at present not speaker-restricted. If that is the issue the answer is that our present speaker-restricted device can have its function so duplicated: the sense of 'I have a headache' may be cumbrously achieved by 'This has a headache', where the second sentence is uttered by a particular speaker who uses further appropriate but manageable gestural conventions such as pointing. Given such added adjustments the differences between these two utterances would be unimportant for our purposes, except for a point to be gone into in the next paragraph. That this identity of function can be achieved is a trivial point and upon it would hinge a trivial dispute for though the reductionist is correct in claiming that he can self-refer with impersonal demonstratives he must admit that he cannot self-refer in the precise way the first person device manages even if he is allowed adjustments to his *im*personal demonstratives. Nevertheless it must be admitted that impersonal devices can achieve self-reference. What we want to see now is the point of those special features of the first person which did not seem to be shared by our impersonal demonstratives even when they were successfully involved in self-reference. We want to see what the point is of the unique way the first person manages self-reference.

It is, by the way, of importance to remember that our first person convention does not operate anything as directly as do our impersonal devices of references. Ordinary demonstratives may be too powerful, their environment too unstructured to serve as exact deputies for our speaker-restricted device. Thus, whoever he is, he is after all speaking as he uses the speaker-restricted device, something which makes a 'description of who "I" is' unnecessary or inappropriate; to discover who 'I' is we must know only who is speaking, not what he looks like, thinks, feels, etc. It is when he stops *speaking*, that 'I' goes out of use for him – not when he stops feeling or stops being a 'subject of consciousness' (unless that involves some covert form of speech), or starts dreaming. These last conditions hold either less or more than is needed to qualify us as users of 'I' – though we are, of course, potential users as long as we are potential speakers. But we may describe potential users as 'him' or 'you': only the speech-actor himself is 'I'. 'I am I', or 'I am me', only *en acte*.

And of course when he speaks he does so with our presumed attention. Speakers get our attention by speaking; objects do not. Surely this is one important way in which our tools of self-reference differ from those of other-reference: the former may normally presume the attention of the hearer already focused upon their object: the speaker. It needn't be denied, of course, that I myself, may still be one topic among many; but for this topic my speaking primes you, as it were, for *I* as speaker already have your attention. I should like now to go further into the special features of the first person.

Suppose we do feel inclined to accept that our self-referential device is not replaceable by other elements of our vocabulary unless these elements are themselves so newly coded that the way in which they are 'replacements' is unimportant. Yet the inclination to accept this ought to prompt us to ask why this rather unique device of the first person with its special features should exist as so elemental an aspect of our speech? I want to try to answer this directly but speculatively now and be allowed adjustments as we go along. The reasons for our hearer-restricted device are more obvious and are not as central for the moment and I shall discuss them later.

What is the function of the first person in the light of its special features?

Let us accept for the moment (a) that a particular case of speech is itself identifiable in the usual ways we identify other actions as yours or mine or his; and (b) that the speaker is also uniquely selectable, just as is any other actor in terms previously and ultimately spatial and temporal; and (c) that our first-person device with its special features left as they are is inextrudible in a non-trivial sense. There then follow certain consequences.

4

First, it is unlikely that the presence in any locution of a speaker-restricted device such as 'my' 'I', or 'mine' will do a referring job at odds with our normal means in these matters: 'Who is speaking?' is a question answerable within these normal demonstrative means. Should we *insist* on sufficiently extraordinary referring work for the above speaker-restricted words we must *ex hypothesi* accept a *sui generis* personal particular, or some covering 'presupposition' within our language.

But if the terms in question do not work as words of identification either at odds with, or obviously by means of, our normal spatial-temporal tools then how do they work? I want to argue that there is in the case of speech an important functional difference between reference and self-reference and the manner in which the self-referential device operates should not require us through fear of incoherence to say there are 'minds' or that there are 'persons' or presuppositions within the language or anything else of that sort, good or bad. Perhaps it is not a bad principle to note that when a view seems incoherent it is not usually because a concept (Person?) or entity (Mind?) needs straightforward adding or presupposing; even less usually, as everyone knows, is it because words we thought might be ordinarily referential turn out to be extraordinarily so. The addition of concepts or entities rarely has made articulate what was not so before; here, in particular, addition is too simple a remedy for what ails us. What often does help an apparent incoherence is the clearer discrimination of a function not yet quite clear.

When we speak it is clear, or can be, who speaks. We have no need for special monograms to mark an utterance as uniquely mine or yours; neither have we need uniquely to mark any other actions of ours to make them each discriminable as our own. Performances take place at a place, at a time; to say that we each perform our own speech actions is a necessary principle for roughly the same reasons as it is to say that each thing has its own position at a time. Actions have a particular place-time roughly for the same reasons that what acts has a particular place-time.

Now any system of communication which allows us such operations as we have in speech will contain topic-introducing devices. The special topics of discourse which interest us here are, the hearer, the third person and the speaker, but for the moment particularly the speaker himself. The device of first person which introduces the speaker himself as topic is unique for it is the only device restricted to that role alone. As we have seen, ordinary demonstratives including proper names, so long as they remain ordinary, cannot do the work of the first person since they would remain also geared for other-reference, and hence not for self-reference alone.

How is this self-reference in speech accomplished? We have seen that the speech act itself is uniquely identifying – no one else at this time at this place could so have acted; 'reference' *via* the act itself would be unique reference. Now, if the question of concern to us is how do we achieve unique *self-reference*, obviously that will be a matter of how we achieve self-reference while in the act of speaking itself (or otherwise acting): *self-reference must occur en acte.*[1] But the speech I am engaged in would be uniquely and necessarily my act and to exploit this unique proprietariness as a basis would allow the achievement of unique self-reference. This is exactly what the first-person device does capitalize upon.

No other referring device of speech makes capital out of the above necessary fact; but then no other referring device need be self-referential in this sense. This, to project the argument for a moment, may be much of the nature of the troublesome asymmetry between the first person and the other two persons – and, if it is, our treatment of that asymmetry and of its previous philosophical and sceptical consequences will undergo some change.

[1] That was why pointing *could* be a complete surrogate for saying 'I': the self-pointer rather than the speaker would be a uniquely identifiable actor if the situation were as carefully structured as is the speaker-hearer situation.

This then, in rough, is my case for the contention that 'I' is peculiarly a device of reference whose utterance or performance itself provides, by the unique proprietariness of such performance, its own basis for that reference. The first person is a device of *performatory reference.* Our conventions are such that to utter 'I . . .' is to refer, by way of that act of utterance itself and its necessary connection to the speaker, to the speaker himself. This, I think, is unique among all expressions of speech; but then so are the requirements of a *general,* interchangeable device of unique self-reference.

It must not be thought in opposition here that there is a 'self' beyond the speaker, as it were, a 'self' further related to the uniqueness-supplying act of speech of which the use of 'I' has made capital. We might wonder, that is, why 'I' must be a speaker-restricted term and is not perhaps (also) a 'self'-restricted one. Or further, why is 'speaker' not a 'self'-restricted expression rather than 'self' a speaker-restricted expression. The answer is the one already given: the only sufficiently unique events to serve as context for a successful *general and interchangeable convention of self-reference in speech* are those of the acts of speech themselves, which, as acts, belong uniquely to the performer himself. No terms, self-referential or otherwise, are in use except as we perform; but the first person, 'I', 'me', 'mine', 'myself', is limited in application as well as use, just to performers; and such bastard self-referential terms as 'a self', 'the self'; 'an I' ought, in being kept in quotes, to indicate their cashability as something like 'the speaker', which is something quite unlike 'I'. When we are not performers the words which uniquely self-select the performer have no function for us or applicability to us, because in that case we cannot, necessarily, be self-referers but only spoken of or spoken to. Also, even when we *are* performers, expressions such as 'the self' are not self-referential and hence do not catch what it is 'to be an I' – if indeed anything could.

13. *The systematically elusive 'I'*

Incidentally, the above way of putting the matter of the first person may help force again but differently into the fire the old philosophical chestnut of 'the systematically elusive I' and perhaps further elucidate our first person device. The puzzle goes something like this. In cases of the use of 'I' such as 'I thought of Moose Jaw yesterday', or even 'I am not six feet tall', there is something forever residual in the 'I' such that 'Who am I?' or 'Who is the I?' are systematically unanswerable since the answer in containing 'I' again will merely raise again the question. There is something forever second-order about 'the self' which is therefore unemptiable, forever elusive. Bergson, among others, might have argued this way and, as a matter of fact, the argument is most pernicious in its epistemological form where it generates such further 'concepts' as 'consciousness of self' or 'awareness of awareness'.

The answer to this construance of the puzzle might, I think, be as follows. The core of the puzzle is that no other expressions may be used only by me of myself; 'I' has no deputies and is itself not a deputy: thus its systematic escape from content: our early suspicions that 'I' is not a pronoun were well founded. And of course it will escape content so long as we continue to search for the wrong sort of filler. 'I' does not 'refer' to any characteristic set of ordinary or extraordinary properties; it is a non-descriptive term. It is a totally translucent referential term operating *via* the proprietary nature of one's speech acts.

Thus to ask 'Who am I?' is in the very use of the first person to have already answered that question to the full limits of that device. It is as if we asked, 'Which question-asker is asking this very question?' and if we cannot answer that question, or rather if it does not answer itself, we are in trouble. And beyond that, 'I' does not take us.

We can, however, see what motivates and sympathize with that frame of mind which makes such misuse of the first person. If we do not know that the speech act, 'I . . .', itself constitutes self-reference *via* the proprietary nature of that act of speech, then we may be tempted to ask to what the first person refers. It refers to the speaker who is uttering 'I'. And beyond that, or more deeply than that, 'closer to the self' than that it does not take us.

III. Personal Pronouns (B)

14. *Which of the special features of the first person are essential to self-reference?*

These features were (i) Only I may use 'I' of myself; (ii) Anyone may use 'I' of himself; (iii) Only the speaker may use 'I' (only) of himself.

(i) *Only I may use 'I' of myself.* There are two facets to this. The first is the necessary and itself unimportant truth that only the self-referrer may refer to himself. This aspect of self-reference we cannot shake. The second is the construction, which comes up again in the third feature, that I may use 'I' *only* of myself; that is, the self-referential device may be (is) used only for self-reference. This as we saw earlier is a non-necessary feature of self-reference; we may perform the function of the first person by pointing or by using proper 'names' which may be used by you of me as *well* as by me of myself. The tool of self-reference needn't limit itself to just that role; and of course the reason it needn't be so limited is that there is not all that difference between self-reference and other-reference. Nevertheless there are economies to limiting our device of self-reference to that role alone.

(ii) *Anyone may use 'I' of himself.* The *generality* of the first person is a highly economic though still inessential characteristic of its function. A 'name' which might allow us self-reference is usable only by one of us of himself while the first person is a single device usable generally by any of us for self-reference.

(iii) *Only the speaker may use 'I' (only) of himself.* This speaker-restricted feature of the first person has three aspects, the first two of which are possibly shared by the first feature. The first aspect is the necessary truth that the self-referrer himself must make the reference; this is the point of the first 'only'. The second aspect, which is the point of the second 'only', is that this particular self-referential device is limited to that work alone. The third and most important aspect suggests that advantage has been taken of the unique proprietariness of a speech action and, that by means of such proprietariness, in conjunction with the fact that the self-referrer must anyhow speak, a *general* economic basis for uniqueness in self-reference is provided. Each speaker does his own speaking. It is important that only the *speaker* may self-refer since advantage is taken of that necessary fact in our conventions of the first person. But advantage needn't have been taken of that fact. When we failed to take such advantage we found ourselves, as in the case of proper names, with an uneconomic set of individual self-referring devices rather than a general such device. One of the main differences between self-reference and other-reference is just that in the latter case we do not have a single purely verbal convention of reference for diverse particulars: we must point or do, or presume something else of that sort *as well as speak.* But for self-references we needn't do more than verbalize, 'I . . .' In our spoken use of the first person we economize by conventionalizing upon the necessary condition of spoken self-reference – the condition that the self-referrer must himself speak. We might have ignored this and have set up many separate, hence uneconomical, conventions of self-reference.

It does seem that all three special features of the first person as a referring device are inessential to the job of self-reference; that perhaps the first person is a specialized way, with perhaps good reason for such results. I want to generalize this point somewhat by looking further at the relations between reference and self-reference.

15. *Reference and self-reference*

If we go about setting up a scheme of self-reference in the uneconomic way suggested by the use of proper 'names' we would find, I have argued, no difference between self-reference and other-reference even down to the ultimate conventions we must employ in achieving both sorts of reference. Such a scheme, if successful, would of course suggest that there are not *two* sorts of reference. I might introduce myself as a topic of discourse just in the way you introduce me or in the way either of us introduces other things as topics of discourse. There isn't a type-difference between my saying successfully of myself, 'Enos is the man standing before you,' and your saying it successfully of me to a third person. Nor is there a type-difference between pointing at oneself and pointing specifically elsewhere. The uniqueness offered by certain descriptions or spatial-temporal orientations will allow us equally to other-refer and self-refer. Part of the reason we may introduce ourselves as topics just as others introduce us is that both such introductions, both self-reference and other-reference, are for others not for ourselves. But this does not mean that a different introduction might then be possible to ourselves: We introduce ourselves *to* others and we introduce other topics, and ourselves as topic, *to* or *for* others; we don't introduce anything *to* ourselves or *for* ourselves.

But what of the case of the first person convention as it is, which allows us the economy of a general convention of self-reference by employing the unique proprietariness of a speech action? In accepting such economy have we changed the ground upon which we make our self-individuations? Do our actions have a different basis of individuation than do material bodies? At first look it might seem so because there is nothing (yet) uniquely proprietary about a particular place-time while there does seem to be something untransferable about one's actions: Someone else might conceivably have been at this place at this time, but it seems no one else could be doing my squinting into the sun in the relevant sense. For someone else to be doing my squinting into the sun he would have to be me, but for someone else to be just here now he needn't be: I could be elsewhere; but I can't be separated from my squinting. This is not a very difficult puzzle. For its solution you need only point out that my squinting goes on at a particular place – that is what is accomplished by the appropriate use of 'my'; and of course a squint already taking place at a particular time, and so identified, cannot be taking place elsewhere or at another time and be the same squint in the relevant sense. Saying 'My squint cannot be someone else's,' is like saying that I cannot be he or this cannot be that. Squints or other actions have no relevant history independent of the history of the individuals of which they are modes and in terms of which they are identified. The reason my squint cannot conceivably be another's is then because there are no identifiable squints without squinters or parts of squinters and no other squinter could be at this place at this time without the previous squinter, me, being at another place at this time. Actions are non-transferable because they get their identity from the spatio-temporal body of which they are modes. In order for them to be transferable the possessing particulars themselves would have to be so; that is, they would have to be non-particulars or non-identities.

In a comparable sense, of course, the particular position of a body at a time is also non-transferable, for that is itself the basis of the uniqueness and proprietariness of an action. *It will then also be the basis upon which self-reference by means of the first person device is achieved.*

I take it therefore that self-reference and other-reference are not two possibilities set on different planes but two possibilities on the same plane. The introduction of oneself as the topic of discourse bears the same relation to the introduction of a material object as the introduction of a material object as topic bears to the introduction of another material object; or, pointing to oneself is as different from pointing to another object as pointing to one object is from pointing at another. There is, I want to say, no particular species of reference which is self-reference and no particular species of reference which is other-reference.

I began with three concurrent questions. I asked whether unique self-reference could be achieved without the use of our first person device as it is. The answer, I think, is that it is so achievable. I asked what then were the nature and point of the special non-necessary features of our present self-referential conventions. My answer was that these special first-person features served an economic function enabling us to work with a *general* and interchangeable single tool of self-reference rather than many such tools. We introduce ourselves as topics automatically, as it were, by means of a single convention based on the proprietariness of speech action and thus dispense with the need of many single self-introductions we would have to perform as alternative. And I have just suggested that if this is how 'I' functions then, despite the asymmetries of the first person, we perform our self-introductions on the same grounds as we perform our other-introductions. This does not seem to me an implication readily acceptable to most sceptics. I asked also in what sense the first person is involved in the formulation of the paradoxes. I found it involved. I want to return to that bit now and look more closely at this involvement of the first person and also to see whether our view of the contingent features of the first person affects the formation of the personal paradoxes.

16. *Is our view of the first person relevant to the alleviation of the paradoxes?*

It seems to me that one important, if not the important, aspect to the personal paradoxes would be contained in the purported difference between self-ascription and other-ascription. The proprietariness and uniqueness of a self-ascription as opposed to an other-ascription produces the rub from which spring the sceptic's claims. These claims are that the two forms of ascription are so essentially different that though we use the same list of epithets for both selves and others there must be some line or other drawn in principle between one kind of use and the other.

I want to suggest that the proprietariness and uniqueness

which is wrongly claimed to be characteristic of some self-ascription, and without which the personal paradoxes cannot stand, are linked to the proprietariness and uniqueness of the first person device as it is.

We can, it seems, make out the unique proprietariness of any personal self-ascription only in link with a self-referential device which is proprietary-making: Only *I* may say that I am in pain; Only *I* may know that I am in pain; *My* pain cannot be *your* pain; *You* cannot in principle have *my* pain, and so on. The 'parallel' between such claims to proprietariness on behalf of a certain class of personal self-ascriptions and the proprietariness afforded just by some of the non-necessary rules of the first person is too close to be ignored: Only I may say 'I' of myself, we remember.

It can be argued,[1] however, that we may insert the required asymmetric proprietariness into our personal ascriptions without using the first person or any other self-referential device. Peter cannot have Paul's pain; (in a sense), only *Paul* may say that he is in pain; (in a sense), only *Paul* may know that he is in pain, and so on.

Now clearly we do not here want to discuss that form of proprietariness which is merely a recitation of the Law of Identity. Here we want before us the sense in which certain, say psychological, states are in a special proprietary fashion apparent to their owners while their, say physical, states are not. When I am in pain I am aware of myself being so in a way which, even if you truly remark it of me, you are not aware of my being so; while when I am coloured brown I may, say see, this of myself only in ways sharable exactly by you if you see it of me. There is nothing apparent to me about my colour which would not be equally apparent to you. It is the epistemological proprietariness of a certain class of cases we want before us, not the proprietariness of identity.

Then I want to ask whether this epistemological proprietariness may be stated without the use, or background use, of a

[1] Both P. F. Strawson and D. Pears so argued.

self-referential device like the first person. The counter-case before us was, Peter may not feel Paul's pain, or, Only Paul may feel Paul's pain. The proprietariness of certain of our states seems utterable with the use of only third person indices or even person-neutral indices rather than *self*-referential ones.

But how could I know that Peter may not feel Paul's pain? After all, that is a crucial question since, 'Peter' and 'Paul', being *ex hypothesi* third person devices, must be in the mouth of another who is thus first person. Why should any of us who are not Peter and not Paul apply the operative words 'only', 'feel' and 'pain' in *such* ways to Peter and Paul? Suppose Paul tells me this of Peter and himself. What form of words, persuasive of this point, could Paul use but: 'Peter may not feel my pain'? This can't help a non-first-person formulation since we are back just with the first person. But unless I can get some such first-person information from Peter and Paul then, *ex hypothesi*, there is no allowable basis for these proprietary other-person claims of mine about Peter and Paul.

It is part of the case, isn't it, that if we are limited solely to other-reference as in the examples before us, such evidence as *would* allow any of us to make a sufficiently proprietary other-person claim by means of, 'Peter cannot feel Paul's pain', is unfortunately enclosed solely between Peter and Paul. And this then bars the speaker from access to what is required for the contrast between those others, those third persons, Peter and Paul. This case which claims we can get the required contrast between selves and others without the implicit force of a self-referential device would then be like solipsism in reverse: there are only others. What we need in order to be allowed to enter the case, to make the troublesome contrast between Peter and Paul, is at least one first-person ascription *contrasted against* an other-ascription. Contrasts among second and third persons alone cannot produce the required epistemological proprietariness: in such a case the predicate in question remains univocal, hence without contrast. The sceptic only begins, contrast starts, when equivocal senses are possible. And equivocal senses become possible only when we introduce the first person qualification of some predicates in contrast to the other-person uses of such predicates. Neither, of course, would contrasts among first-persons alone do. Both selves and others are needed, not just others and not just selves.

If both are needed to make the case for troublesome epistemological proprietariness it is yet 'the self' which is naturally vested, or expected to be, with the epistemological 'extra'. That is perhaps why Wittgenstein, just to avoid this non-transferably-owned extra, is willing to say that some uses of 'I' are not (self-)referential at all. Surely it is at least partly why Descartes would settle for two disparate senses for 'I'; and possibly why Strawson feels that since criteria of self-ascription (the 'extra') do seem to differ from those of other-ascription, the concept of a Person or 'Self-plus-Other' is thus implied to lend coherence to predicates used with this otherwise systematic difference: Persons are what allow the meanings of such predicates to be the same even though their criteria of ascription seem to differ from first- to other-person cases.

Surely it will be the case that a view which finds certain personal predicates to be, on pain of paradox, or incompleteness, type-distinct from impersonal ones will also feel the need for a type-distinct or type-proprietary personal demonstrative. It would hence be important to show whether or not our personal demonstratives are type-distinct, that is, whether or not they function differently from our impersonal demonstratives. Moreover, whatever reason is found for such a view about personal predicates, that view in its statement will still need the contrast between the first and the other persons, as I have tried to argue. And if one can show that our main tool of self-reference is only misleadingly a different type of index from our impersonal demonstratives we shall perhaps have removed at least one of the bases for such statable contrast between selves and others. *Is* the contrast between personal and impersonal predicates really separate from the contrast between selves and others? And is this separate from the contrast between 'I' and 'he'?

We have then a strong and a weak case to be made at this point for the utility of working upon our personal demonstratives, and in particular, upon the personal pronouns, which afford the crucial means of distinction between ourselves and others. Proper names, and other such personal demonstratives, we saw, allow us only the distinction among others, hence we cannot avoid the need to take into account our tools of self-reference. The strong case then would be that the operation of our means of distinction between selves and others is as good a point to *test* the role of the notion of a Person as any, given the consistency of that set of concepts.

Should, for instance, a sceptical view be held about the possibility of knowing what other minds know then we have in consistency a right to expect a contrast among our personal demonstratives which will reflect that epistemological scepticism. 'I' would have to be somehow systematically different from other demonstratives to support the epistemological difference of the self. Hence the first-person device will have to perform its demonstrations in a manner typically different from our other-person devices or our impersonal devices of reference. How could we otherwise form our sceptically-minded sentences?

Or should, for example, the view be that personal verbs are category-different from material-object verbs, then this category difference too must be reflected among our personal demonstratives: how else could the *verb* still be category-different? And if we could show our personal demonstratives to be not category-different or not sceptic-productive, then by *modus tollens* we might show any such contrast views to be mistaken. It is this lack of contrast between our personal and impersonal demonstratives, this lack of type-proprietariness in our first person, its normalcy, that I hope to have suggested to this point. Of course, this cannot mean the work is done. We must still show that this absence of category-difference among our personal demonstratives is truly reflected among our personal predicates. Reflection can be reversible. We shall also want to see what some of the temptations are to move us to hold out a category-difference for our personal predicates and to see that they are not actually more than temptations.

The weak view about the importance of our personal demonstratives for the problem of Persons is that the contrast between our use of the first person and the other persons is by itself a direct source of temptation to an asymmetric perspective between selves and others. It would then be useful to block off those avenues misleadingly suggested by the actual aberrations of the special features of the first person. It would be useful to show that the first person is only misleadingly not a normal demonstrative: its special features are not special enough problematically to contrast selves with others. I have tried to show something of how we might take this to be the case. But to have done this would be only to have closed off one misleading approach which, on the weak view, holds no implication for the success or failure of any other approach.

17. *Speaker-hearer asymmetry*

I should like next to come at this question of the asymmetry of the first person by setting it alongside the other persons. I hope to show that the second person is as asymmetrical a phenomenon as is the first person – that there is a symmetrical asymmetry between them. This argument might then serve as a *reductio* of the position which finds the self asymmetrically placed. That is, one way of illustrating the nature of the bond between the first and second person is to show the unexpected symmetry that lies between 'I' and 'you' as regards their power of producing the personal paradoxes. This would be to show that 'you' is as strange as 'I' or that 'I' is as unproblematic as 'you'.

It is normally thought that the difficulties we have with our notion of persons comes at the division a sceptic might attempt to force between selves and others. The cut, it is normally held, comes between 'I' and the other personal pronouns. The force behind the positioning of this cut, we saw, was 'I''s seeming asymmetry to the other personal pronouns, indeed, to all other comparable expressions: no on else may use 'I' of me and thus no noun can satisfy the pronominal nature of 'I'; this is not to mention the not independent matter of the apparent epistemological differences of the first person which I shall discuss in Chapters VI and VII.

But it is equally tempting to argue that there are at least occasions upon which no noun will satisfy the pronominal nature of 'you'. This would require sceptical cuts not only between 'I' and 'you' but also between 'you' and 'others' and so on. Let us run a test on whether 'you' is an unsatisfiable pronoun. Obviously we may say either, 'Enos come here' or 'You come here' with comparable results and within only slightly differing situations, but it may be said that 'you' is 'understood' in the first case and thus is not replaced by 'Enos'. Independently, however, of how we treat such examples there are still normal cases of confrontation between a speaker and a hearer where 'you' is not without oddity replaceable by some deputy expression unless, of course, we newly conventionalize that deputy to mark it as hearer-restricted. 'You're tired' or 'Enos, you're tired' are neither of them construable within the limits of 'Enos is tired' unless, again, we assume, or, there is a family code, that Enos is spoken *to* in this way.

Still, however it is done, we want to be able to distinguish cases of speaking to someone from those of speaking of someone. Context alone cannot do that for us unless it is aided by some conventionalized addition to itself. Our use of 'you' happens to be that conventionalized addition. And of course it does not itself mean something like 'the person addressed' for even this normally third-person expression would have to be suitably coded to achieve hearer-restriction. In fact, just as it was true of 'I', no translation will do for 'you'.

On this score, then, our speaker-restricted and hearer-restricted conventions are identical and that is why it is possible to say of both of them that they are in some of their cases unsatisfiable by any uncoded noun replacements. They are more like pure speech operators. When we thought this was true only of 'I' there seemed grounds for the special asymmetry of the first person: Only I may use 'I' of myself; 'I' is not replaceable by any description. But this is true of both 'I' and 'you': only 'you' may be used of you; 'you' is not replaceable by any description. 'He' will have similar although not identical eccentricities. We have here then either the *reductio* option of accepting 'me', 'you' and 'him' as all somehow sceptically impenetrable, each by the other: this is the same choice as countenancing three senses to our personal pronouns; or we have the choice of seeing these personal pronouns as operative at a task other than heretofore thought. Something else must explain their operations than the view which treats any of them as primarily part of an epistemological or subjectively motivated classification which results in the peculiar asymmetric placing of the first person.

18. *Symmetrical asymmetry among all three persons*

I want now to turn from the grammatical to a preliminary epistemological aspect and ask whether we do, as has been normally thought, have unique grounds for saying what we do only in those cases where we correctly use the first personal pronoun; or do we employ different grounds in *each* of the three pronoun uses? Does the epistemological aspect run parallel with and reinforce the grammatical aspect of the three persons? This will be the same as to ask whether, as is usually held, the epistemological cut comes between 'I' and the others or whether there is also something unique about the way in which each of the other two grammatical persons is allowed to yield its information.

Suppose there is a speaker, someone spoken to, and someone spoken of; and suppose for the moment, what is not the case, that I and you and he play out only that role with which we begin. The shifts among these roles I shall discuss later.

He, *ex hypothesi*, is neither speaker nor spoken to and, if we accept the universalizability of the speech model as regards communication, he is also barred from entering into other forms of conventionalized communication, such as gestural, with you and me. On the question of the function of personal pronoun distinction, the speech model will embrace any other communication model as a case in point. As the person spoken of he cannot then trade on conventions without going beyond the bounds of his role. We learn what we do of him, *qua* him, by what he may be doing, or may do, or from what others may report of these things.

But they may not report his speech as such among his other activities, for then we learn, albeit by hearsay, from him and not of him. To have learned from him that he was at the University of Chicago's squash courts is to have allowed him the additional role of a speaker and so to have given him a dual role which would have to be factored. Only in his capacity as an 'I' may we have learned from him that he was at the courts. As a 'he', he is insurmountably mute and we accordingly confined in our knowledge of him.

As for you, obviously I may observe you in the same way as I may him; but you, as hearer or person spoken to without limitation of topic, may be *told* what I see of you and thus encouraged, aided, guided, commanded and so on. And there will occur obvious feedback effects of and on your behaviour, among them as we shall see, that of speech response itself. None of this interplay for the moment could be true with him though he may react to my presence as if he anticipated such comment. He is less the third person, however, the more even such tacit interplay develops between us. One-way glass is not used without good reason by psychologists.

There is a less obvious epistemological difference between the third, and the second person already alluded to above in the mention of speech response itself as a kind of behaviour elicited from the hearer. There are, that is, speech forms which hinge their success upon the requirement that the person addressed shall speak or conventionally respond or perform, if you like, as an 'I'. There are, for the most obvious reasons, no comparable speech forms which so involve the third person that he need in his role respond to his discussors to insure the operation of those speech forms themselves which treat him as third person.

But there are just such speech forms which might be called uniquely second person in their direction. Why should questions, for instance, be so hearer-restricted? They are so because of the necessary and trivial facts that the person from whom the speech response is desired must be one and the same with the person to whom I speak. We are limited of whom we may ask questions because questions must be necessarily put or spoken or otherwise signalled before they are such; and once they are such the second person convention must take hold for its function is to indicate that this is hearer-addressed as must indeed any utterance be. The reason our second person devices have become tacit or 'understood' in many interrogative situations is because we have also the primary question device of pitch itself which signals a response is expected – and from whom else could it be so expected but from you?

Thus to say that I may ask a question only of a 'you' is only to say the trivial and necessary thing that if speech is the question's only vehicle then the question must be addressed and, *ex hypothesi*, only a 'you', a person addressed, could be its addressee. We do ask 'Will he tell me?' but this is not on a par with 'Will you tell me?' since the first is not addressed to him and may serve only as an ellipsis for, 'Can you tell me whether he will tell me?' And of course, questions which you carry for me to another are only irrelevantly troublesome.

The further matter of what assurances you in particular have that you are the questioned individual is explained by the conventions of context we may select as we query: looking at the person you will question, or knowing and calling his name, or pointing, or using an individuating description, and so on. In all these cases we are powerfully aided by a special preparedness we all have to attend to the speech of others, especially when certain intonation contours are used.

Should these points be true, we have before us a crucial, or if you like logical, difference between the second and third persons. Second persons may be required to speak in a sense of 'require' which could not be true of third persons. Of course any third person may speak, an important fact, but the moment he does so he has transgressed his role. And although we might request him to speak, or question him, this too would already have required a transgression of this 'thirdness' and a move into 'secondness'. If, as I say, this is true then it seems we have epistemological access to 'you' in a way we cannot have it of 'him'.

Our grounds for saying what we do of third persons then appear different than our grounds for saying what we do of second persons, and, presuming for the moment that we have different grounds for saying what we do as first person, we are presented reason to separate all three persons each from the other rather than reason only to separate the first person off from the others.

Should we offer a sceptic this bait he would find several reasons to reject it. (a) He could say 'you' and 'he' may, as a matter of fact, interchange roles so that there is between them no systematic or sceptical separation. (b) Or he could say that any means I may have of learning something of you are still also means available to me in my own case but not *vice versa*. (c) There is still a sense in which I remain an 'I' or remain myself even when I too become, as I may, a 'you' or a 'he'.

But of course the bait was meant all along to be unpalatable for the sceptic. We hoped to find ourselves in a position where the sceptic's treatment of the first person as unique is just as unpalatable as treating the second and third persons each as unique. I want to say something, then, about why the sceptic's reasons for rejecting the proffered extension of his position to second and third person cases are good reasons but too good for him to use.

(a) Only in the case where we artificially set up restrictions of movement from role to role in order to observe the limits of each could it begin to seem in the least, or philosophically, appealing to see the uniqueness of a 'you' as opposed to a 'him'. But these restrictions of movement from role to role must necessarily be artificial since, as we have seen, it is at least part of the role of the person spoken to that he may be called upon to speak. There is equally no barrier to the third person becoming second person. Anyone or anything within certain contingent capability limits may be spoken to, and what may be spoken to may be spoken of, though not always the reverse. This lack of bounds upon conversion from 'you' to 'he' means there are no epistemological gaps between the second and third persons which may not be filled by either speaking to or speaking of the individual in question. Cases where we are able to speak of an object, say a squash ball, and cannot speak to it, are cases where a distinction is needed; that is why we have available, within the third person, the devices 'he' and 'it'. But we have obviously no need for it in the second person. For these good reasons of potential conversion among at least the last two persons, the sceptic need not accept the *reductio* offered him of creating a scepticism or division in principle among all three persons.

For the same good reasons, however, he will find it difficult to restrict full freedom of movement not merely between the second and third but among all three persons. Anyone or anything within certain contingent capacity limits may become a speaker and certainly anyone capable of being a hearer may on occasion be the speaker. Hence even should we accept the unique function of some aspects of all three persons there is no reason, but rather the reverse, to expect all three functions may not at various times be fulfilled by the same individual. We cannot, at least on the face of it, expect an openness to conversion among two of these personal aspects and not the third.

(b) Perhaps, however, the scale between the three persons seems changed only on the face of it and the old scale still holds essentially. The old scale was that any means available to me in my assessment of you are also available to me in my own case but not *vice versa.* I see, the example goes, the position of your limbs and I may, perhaps not quite as easily, see the position of my own as well; but I may also assess where mine are kinaesthetically, etc., and this is something I cannot quite do of yours. I am denied means in your case which I have for mine, but any means available to me for your case are also available to me for mine.

This is just not so. It is mistaken to think that any means available to me in my assessments of you are also available to me in my self-assessments. Later in Chapter VI, I hope to provide reasons for allowing it to be said that what*ever* means are available to the first person are also available to the second and third persons; but for the moment I am only meeting the sceptic on his own quixotic ground.

I may question you and be answered, or you may just volunteer information. Such means are unavailable to me in my own case. The question of whether I could actually make use of such information for my own case is irrelevant since what is being argued is whether the scale of means available for self- and other-assessment is merely a diminishing one as we go from ourselves to others. The above exception and its implications establish that there are means available to me in my assessment of you which are not available to me in my assessment of myself: I don't volunteer information to myself nor do I informatively answer my own questions provided they are questions and not deliberations, musings, hypotheses or other problematic but non-interrogative forms.[1] More fully, I just don't speak 'to' myself in anything like the way you speak to me and all the information about you, direct and indirect, available to me in your speech is absent, *ex hypothesi*, in my speech whether it is addressed to you or 'to' myself. Even if I monitor my own speech it could not be like listening to yours. I can't miss or be ignorant of all the things I am in the act of

[1] Can you be your own hearer or interviewee, can you address or question yourself? Why should these be different than: can you, without legal weaseling, be your own customer, can you sell to yourself?

saying, but I could have missed or be ignorant of all of what you are saying to me.

The point of this is to keep in symmetrical perspective the differences between the first and the other persons. Should we accept, on whatever grounds, that I have some evidence for saying things about myself, which I cannot have for saying these same things about you, we should be committed also, on the same grounds which I am not at the moment evaluating, to accept the turnabout that I have some evidence for saying things about you, namely from your speech to me, which I cannot have for saying these things about myself. When you tell me you are depressed this is a genre of evidence I cannot have available in my own case since my utterance that I'm depressed cannot, as I say it to you, be evidence to me in the sense in which it might be to you that I am in such a state. Nor would it be evidence to me that I am in such a state were it sensible to believe that I could tell myself so since it is unlikely that telling myself so could add to what I already knew; and realization is not itself evidence – if 'evidence' is the word we want here.

There seems then to be an asymmetrical symmetry between the first and second person as regards evidence for 'ascription'. In each case we seem to have available grounds which are unavailable for the other grammatical person. These grounds, to put it crudely, are feelings, let us say, and being spoken to, respectively. We should then want to say that only I can have my feelings and *also* that only you (or he) can speak to me. Thus the epistemological asymmetry of the first person seems matched by that of the second (and third).

(c) If a sceptic is to make a stand then for the asymmetrical nature of the first person he must do it on grounds other than epistemological and grammatical differences lest he find the other two persons camped symmetrically alongside him. Surely the import of the grammatical and the epistemological symmetries so far argued among all three persons was to remove any hope of a foothold at the top. We must hear new argument from the sceptic if he is to still claim a relevant first person asymmetry.

But such argument since it cannot be new in form is predictable. There is, he will say, one role we may not wander in and out of as we may while in the roles of third or second person. That is the role of self or first person. Even as we function in second and third person roles one's underlying role as first person is co-present. I am never *just* someone spoken to or about but also always myself; never merely a 'you' or a 'he' but always an 'I' or an 'I-as-you' or an 'I-as-he'. Here is the old asymmetry back again, but, I think, attenuated further than it has been.

In order for this present favouring of the 'I' to go forward we must have reasons from which to argue that any second or third person use always presupposes such an underriding first person use; and these reasons must also argue against the converse of this. We must have reasons, for example, why it could *not* be held that you are never just someone spoken of or speaking, but also always you: never merely an 'I' or a 'he' but always a 'you' or a 'you-as-I' or a 'you-as-he' and so on. Perhaps the reason is that I am not always spoken of or spoken to; but, hopefully, *neither need I always be speaking*.

The argument will predictably return to epistemological differences among the persons: I may know what I know of myself in a way unique to me. But there is the counter: I may also know what I know of you in a way unique to you. Yes, but 'I myself, me, I know that I am in pain, if it comes to that, I feel it, in a way *you* cannot'. But this may be a harmless *ex hypothesi* 'cannot' predicated upon the distinction already at hand between 'I' and 'you' as separately identifiable individuals, or as speaker and as hearer, but not as epistemological separates. It need not be meant, as we have seen, that the predicates themselves are always particularized, that couldn't be meant.

Does it mean the speaker has different grounds for himself than he could possibly have for your case? Suppose it does; and suppose we let 'grounds' pass for the moment. But, as we've seen, the speaker has different grounds for judgment of your case than he could possibly have in his own. The asymmetry is symmetrical.

It won't do to counter here that the speaker has no need to speak to himself since what speech might convey he already knows of himself. Thus the asymmetry of the second person would be denied: the first person situation still has available all the second person case has and the second nothing that the first has not. The trouble is that this move presumes a relationship between speech and certain events within the speaker such that I could know, if you spoke, what the nature of those related events was, and hence, could show the irrelevance of speaking to myself as a requirement of matching the second person case. But if the sceptic had available in the first place a trustworthy relationship between speech and, say, inner events then the first person could not maintain its asymmetrical position at all. It was the very unavailability of these inner events to another upon which that asymmetry originally rested.

There is a further difficulty with this present favouring of the first person on epistemological grounds. Something must be said about whether your grounds for yourself, for your use of the first person, may or may not be different than his grounds for his own use of the first person or my grounds for my own use of it. The asymmetrist or sceptic must admit that my own first person grounds may or may not be different from anyone else's first person grounds, including his own, since that ignorance is the sceptic's point about my first person grounds and will thus need to be his point about anyone's first person grounds. But if the sceptic is on his own terms logically barred from both alternates of whether my first person grounds are or are not different from others' first person grounds, including his own, then neither may he sit *between* these as alternates since they are no longer alternatives; he is barred from cogently stating the alternative as incorporating a live option and hence from cashing in, as he must, on a hesitancy as between alternatives. This is related to the point of section 5. In short, if we are tough at the beginning, he cannot articulate the view that the first person is epistemologically asymmetrical since his own position prevents him from saying whether *or* not his grounds are either unique among or similar to others'.

The main argument I offered against the first-person asymmetrist was in the form of a *reductio*. In that instance we take a non-tough line and grant that the first-person grounds of ascription do exhibit some cogent difference and that these differences are not available to second and third persons. If we suppose this, we may ask whether such first-person asymmetry is systematically met by the fact that our second person grounds have about them some cogent difference which is not available as first or third person grounds. I have already argued in favour of this symmetrical asymmetry between first and second person. Any implication to be drawn then as regards the admission that the first person has different grounds for speaking about himself than he could possibly have for speaking about you will also have to be drawn from the parallel admission we must make about the uniqueness of second person grounds, and, perhaps, those of the third person. It is true we have an asymmetry among the three persons, but it is a relevantly symmetrical asymmetry.

But this symmetrical difference as we play the second person role does not prevent our appearance in other roles or make it the master role; nor should the difference of the first person role prevent our appearance in other roles or promote their subservience. There is so far no reason to accept any of the three roles as so characterized that its directions never permit its absence from the stage. Nor has anything been said which could be taken as the claim that any human may not know all that another knows and in precisely the same way. As a matter of fact, the claim that there is total epistemological symmetry among all three persons is just the line I shall support in Chapter VI.

Yet, after all, isn't everything presented to the first person – they are his grounds for saying things of himself, his grounds for saying things of you, or of him? Isn't this the sense in which the self or the 'I' is always on stage? But this too seems to work in any person: all personal predicates come ready to work in three persons so that it could be either 'his grounds', 'your grounds' or 'my grounds' which is the operative phrase. Still, when we feel that his grounds, or your grounds, are nevertheless being presented to me, isn't this feel for the ever-presence of a first-person due to the fact that someone, the first person, must have *expressed* or said, that there were such and such reasons for saying, say, that Enos is hungry? The first person, some first person, must be taken to have said or expressed *whatever* we shall discuss. This is how we table what we discuss: *some*one says it. We do of course say, 'he said . . .' or 'you said . . .' but each of these is itself being said – it is as if we should preface *every*thing said by, 'I say . . .'. We don't, however, need this ubiquitous preface since the act of saying what we say itself mostly serves as this preface each time we speak. We make our own noises and that's a convenient fact to conventionalize upon. Here perhaps we are ready to set an early limit to an epistemological approach to the self and the personal paradoxes.

Questions such as 'Under which condition am I a "self" or an "I"?' or 'When am I first person?' have sometimes been answered in terms of 'consciousness' or 'experience' or 'thinking' or their cognates. But to be an 'I', or a 'self', one need *only* be speaking or using the first personal pronoun without, of course, any form of quotation convention being in effect; nothing more. The present performance of speech is the only necessary condition for the use of the first person although there are plenty of over-necessary conditions. Only when one is actually in the act of speaking, or its derivatives, is one ever capable of being a 'self' or an 'I'. But one is in the act whether one is referring or self-referring. Hence the lack of difference; hence the symmetry.

I hope in the last two chapters to have done two main things. First, to have removed some of the grammatical or logical reasons for the view which type-separates off the first person from the other two. I tried to do this by showing that, given the proprietariness of a speech act, which must, of course, occur as we self-refer, our convention of self-reference has taken advantage to construct a highly economical, general, single-word device wherewith we may all refer to our diverse selves. But there were no substantive differences between referring and self-referring and hence no substantive content to the very real grammatical asymmetry of the first person. Thus if the first person *was* involved as a needed contrast for the statement of at least some of the personal paradoxes then such statement is now hindered by the absence of such effective contrast.

Second, I hope to have removed some of the epistemological disproportions of the first person by arguing that *such* disproportion might equally be made out at least for the second person. But this was really only to have argued the penalties of such disproportion. In Chapters V and VI I hope to be able to show something of the more proper epistemological proportions between ourselves and others.

IV. Private Language

19. *Systematically private language*

A question which at several points may have seemed to have been waiting is whether systematically private 'speech' or 'language' (SPL) is possible. No one, of course, will argue whether language could be private in a non-systematic sense, whether, for instance, Robinson, alone on his island, could or would develop his own language. That kind of speculation sets only contingent limits to the notion of speech; we are interested in the makings of more necessary limits: would it still be 'speech' or 'language' if in principle only I could use it, if no one else could, in principle, understand certain aspects of it.

Actually I shall also be arguing the question of the possibility of a systematically private language when I argue the business of speech acts and systematically ulterior motives in Chapter V. Here I hope to come at the matter of SPL from another perspective making direct use of those aspects of the first-person which may bear on this matter.

As I've said, the issue worth arguing is not whether I alone on an island, without the stimulus of another might unpragmatically develop a 'language' or system of notation such as notches on the palm tree; the issue is not whether a hearer *is* actually involved but whether he is involv*able* or introduce-*able*. In some ways these two, the worthy and the unworthy of argument, do come together; indeed the latter, as I hope to show, is a necessary condition of the former in the sense that the presence of others must be schemed for all along. At any rate I think, to make the issue of a systematically private language philosophically of interest, and germane here, we need to begin somewhat down the line and ask not whether that notion is articulate, for clearly it isn't, but why it is not. Let me draw out then a presupposition or two sunk, I think, into any description of an SPL in order to work toward this end.

20. *The necessity of the first person to private language*

I think it is plain that no arguments for an SPL could gain even the slightest momentum without the appearance of the kind of distinction marked by the first personal pronoun; the first person or something just like it is a necessary condition to the purported statement of the possibility of an SPL. This, for at least two related reasons. First, only the grammar of 'I' seems capable of supporting the required sense of 'systematic'; indeed 'systematically' in the phrase 'systematically private' *must* take its power from 'my' since any demonstrative term which might otherwise fit the locution, such as 'your' or 'his' or even 'this', would clearly involve a non-systematic sense of privacy unless we insisted in those cases too on the necessity of harking back to 'the self' as touchstone. But this move would leave us again with the first person. It is the seeming 'non-transferable' aspect of *first* person ascriptions which anyway motivates the entire matter. In other words, only 'I' seems sufficiently asymmetrical from all other demonstratives to yield in conjunction with a predicate or predicate noun a sense which would be systematically asymmetric to any other senses or uses of those predicates. And this form of asymmetry is precisely what SPL needs: it is another form of misconceiving, I think, the asymmetry of the first person. We tend, partly, to think that just as I may use 'I' only of myself there are certain attributions or utterances which I may make only of myself.

A second reason for the indispensability of the first person to SPL is that the language must be usable by only one 'speaker', as it were. There must, that is, be available a means of stating the required systematic *limitation of users* to the 'current' user; and the only device which will even seem to allow this to be stated is the first person: Only *I* may use (understand, etc.) this language; only *I* may know what I mean by 'anxiety'.

21. *Arguments not to be used*

Now I do not want to argue here that there cannot occur this required sense of 'only', that since 'only' is an exceptive, it consequently cannot operate except as restrictive upon a group of possible candidates while in the case before us the very thing we are trying to say is precisely that on principle there cannot be any other candidates, that the first person is, in some of its aspects at least, absolutely unique or in principle restricted or exceptional.

Nor do I want to argue that the grammar of 'I' seems not the *only* grammar capable of supporting the required sense of 'systematic asymmetry'. I have already argued that the sense in which 'I' is asymmetric is counterweighed by the asymmetry of 'you'. Thus if there is a language which 'only I' can use there is an apposite sense in which there is a language 'only you' can use. But I do not particularly want to ride on the obvious incoherence of this beyond suggesting that there could be no way of my knowing that there is a language which on principle only you could use. To argue as we might try, from my case to yours, even supposing that my case was acceptable as a case in point, is prohibited if the uniqueness of my own case, i.e. its service as a case in point, is itself to be preserved.

Nor, finally, shall I argue, what must follow anyway from the above, that there can be no sense of the first person hardy enough to stand as uniquely alone as it must stand to allow sense to be made of SPL.

What I shall argue is that the first person is, in a sense, an utterance asymmetric to every other but that its asymmetry has none, I think, of the implications usually made out, nor more especially, does it entail any epistemological idiosyncrasies such as are at the root of SPL or other related 'personal' conundra. This form of argument is not strictly negative and thus only symptomatic of the difficulty. We know we oughtn't to say what SPL seems to say – what we want is to know what to say about the asymmetry of the first person as it connects with SPL.

22. *The relevant nature of first person asymmetry*

I take the following things now for granted. First, that the first person convention is translatable into other of our indexical conventions. But only the first person achieves self-reference in a way which is so economical and general for speech.

We saw earlier that such a general device of self-reference as the first person would have to tie into the individuating aspect of the speech situation in order to attain such width of function, in order, that is, that anyone in the speech situation could use it. This general individual aspect of the speech situation could not be its spatial and temporal features alone, as things stand, though we have seen the sense in which they *could* be. The general individuating aspect of the speech situation which does serve is that speakers do their own speaking in a necessary enough sense to provide us with unique individuation, or rather, self-individuation. When the particular speech act itself contains a device such as the first person, then unique self-reference is achieved and may so be *generally* achieved; and, we remember this accounts for the fact that only the *speaker* may use 'I' (only) of himself.

The following three facts then, argued earlier in Chapter II, are crucial and essential to the function of the first person and consequently unique enough among the rules which govern all other indexical expressions to have illicited the most unique of theories; but these three unique facts are explained on grounds of speech economics, not on unique metaphysical or epistemological grounds. These three facts were, we remember, (a) that only I may say 'I' of myself; (b) Only *the speaker* may say 'I' (only) of himself, and (c) anyone may use 'I' of himself. The first of these in tension with the last produces the balance of *a priori* power characteristic of our usual approach to other minds and persons: how are we to account for the fact that while anyone may use 'I' of himself, still, each of us may use it only of himself alone. The middle feature, I think, is the means of approach between the other two.

The general use of the first person is, of course, easily accounted for. It is a straighforward matter of a contingent choice between simplicity and multiplicity where the same end would be achieved in either case. But the manner in which such generality and simplicity in the first person device is achievable proves a lead to the point of the restriction on its use such that I may use it only of myself. The general and uniquely individuating use of the first person was allowed for by the features of the speech situation that only the speaker speaks his speech and each self-referrer must speak. This is why it is only the speaker who may use 'I' (only) of himself, for the use of 'I' is constructed to be involved uniquely with his proprietary speech act; and it is *via* that restriction of the use of the first person to the speaker that he achieves with it unique self-reference. Thus the *speaker*-restrictedness of our first person device. And thus why only I may say 'I' only of myself – for no other expression except one limited to the speaker *qua* actor could with generality achieve unique self-reference. It is worth noting in this connexion how close to each other in form (and context) are the two necessary truths that 'only I may say "I" of myself' and 'only I may perform my speech acts'.

But for the above dynamics to function we have no need for an additional dimension of reference to accommodate the matter of self-reference, unless, that is, we mistakenly feel that action is already such an additional dimension. There is, however, no justification for such a feeling. Self-reference with the first person is no more mysterious than other-reference though it does have the extra involution mentioned above; actually, self-reference or self-individuation already presupposes ordinary spatio-temporal reference or individuation. I want briefly to argue for this by now obvious relation.

23. *Self-individuation presupposes non-self-individuation*

It seems to me that all that need be said on this score can be said within the confines of whether actions, in our case speech actions, are individuable by the same means we ordinarily and ultimately individuate spatio-temporal particulars. I have already made this point earlier and shall not dwell on it overly now.

The grammatical way of making the point is to remind ourselves that 'action' is a rather high-level general term whose particular cases are always to be found in verb form or with a verb buried in them as with predicate adjectives. But our verbs are always link terms. It is their link with uniquely referring expressions, in cases where individuation is relevant, which allows us to say where and when the action took place. This may not on the face of it seem to be so, as with locutions such as 'The fight began at 9 p.m.' or 'The meeting was over before evening'. But the cases where such utterances have a use are cases where too much is already understood for these utterances to be treated independently. When we understand all of the setting required for the success of these utterances we know enough about the fight and the meeting to answer such questions as who or what is fighting or meeting. And when we do not know the answers to such questions we are entitled to them. In any case, should we come to ask 'which fight?' or 'what meeting?' the orienting answer must come in terms of ordinary particulars, for without such help, covert or otherwise, 'the fight' and 'the meeting' are not, as anyone would agree, uniquely individuating utterances. Where, to reverse the situation, it seems that the performance or action is the uniquely individuating feature of some particular, as in cases such as – 'Which boxer?'; 'The one coming through the ropes' – it is rather that the action individuates since it focuses us on a particular place at a particular time, but not on an empty place, though it may be empty now.

It is this aspect of actions, their occurring at a place at a time, but not at an empty place, which makes them uniquely individuating. It is in this sense that we may say that self-reference presupposes, or at least adds no new dimension to, ordinary spatial-temporal individuation; – at least as regards individuation. But individuation is just the business of our first person convention.

24. *The first person over-burdens private language*

Well, what does all this show about our temptations toward SPL? First of all, I think, it accounts for the asymmetry of the first personal pronoun in a way which pre-empts its abnormal implications. The fact that only I may use 'I' of myself has its explanation in the self-individuating use we make of our proprietary speech action. It is true that no other expression, demonstrative or otherwise, has this feature to it and this does constitute a *bona fide* asymmetry. But its explanation in terms of the economics of self-reference in speech drains it of exactly that feature, always covered with mist anyway, which SPL needed in order to establish its kind of asymmetric point. Let me put this another way.

If it is true that the point of SPL cannot be articulated without the use of the first person device and, revealingly, some limiting term such as 'only', then some locution close to the form of 'Only I may use (understand, etc.), this language' must stand as test for the coherence of the position. And of course it is the hope in such an utterance that the function of the first person is idiosyncratic enough not originally to emburden the position with what it wishes to deny. But this is precisely what is done since the first person, asymmetric though it is, already is involved in normal spatio-temporal, or 'public' if you like, individuation and not some more idio-centred form of individuation. And once you are entitled to introduce your*self* in this way there is no way of keeping out others – whether or not they are speakers. Where we so introduce ourselves as topic then it can only be a contingent fact that others are not so introduceable. Self-introduction is not on a different logical plane from other-introduction. The differences between self- and other-individuation are the differences in the use we make of the speech act itself in self-individuation; but this is not a *sui generis* or type-distinct step. The mysteries of self-reference are no deeper than those of other-reference.

It needn't be added, except parenthetically, that self-individuation is not *for* oneself but for the hearer – if we never spoke to others, or took demonstrative action, there would be no need for the first person, for *I* always know when I'm talking about myself without the advantage of the first person device as signpost. In this naive sense the use of the first person presupposes a hearer. And if SPL presupposes a use for the first person then it presupposes what it hopes to deny – a hearer.

V. Epistemology (A)

25. *An undercutting question*

Although we may feel the sceptic's asymmetrical scaling of selves and others is somehow askew, as in section 18, we do reject with less hesitancy a perhaps more basic measure of his. That measure is the epistemological one that in some sense I am licensed to say certain things of myself such that the same license is denied me should I say these things of another. I have argued that even should we accept this we need not accept the separation off of the first person unless, as is fantastic, we are to accept equally the symmetrical separation of all three persons. We may accept as a canon that the first, second, and third person roles *must* all be fully interchangeable roles without any residual 'personal' trailings as far as the functions of the roles themselves are concerned. But I want anyway now to examine the epistemological root of the first person asymmetry since the *reductio* which results in accepting fully its consequences serves only as a symptom that all is not being said as it should be said.

I want to manœuvre first by temporarily undercutting what has been the traditional question here, namely, 'How do I know that I'm x?' where the values for 'x' are such expressions as 'tired', 'elated', 'depressed', 'hopeful', and, of course, 'in pain', etc. Naturally I hope the new question to be answerable in a way which will help shed some light on the older question. The question I want to introduce is, 'Why should I *say* that I'm x?'. It belongs here for several reasons. First, if it were not the case that others on occasion say of themselves what I have said of myself or that what I say of myself I sometimes say of you or what you sometimes say of yourself you also sometimes say of me – did such contrasts not exist we should have no occasion to contrast the putatively special first-personal sense of 'know' with the other-personal senses of 'know'. In short, 'How do I know that I'm x' is meant to bring out the *contrast* between itself and either 'How do you know that I'm x?' or 'How do I know that you're x?', or both.

Now, if on occasion at least, I did not say I was x, or someone could not *say* they were so, we should have no use at all for the locution 'I am x'. For it to have a use it must occur in the mouth of the speaker. (And when it is used sub-vocally by a speaker it may, so it is said, be so used only because it may be used vocally.) Yet without a use for that locution the contrast between myself and others cannot be made. Thus, one of the conditions for the setting of the epistemological asymmetry between the first and the other two persons is that whatever it is we may claim to know in a special first-person sense must itself follow the conditions of the utterable. If I say you are elated you needn't be saying anything, but for the expression 'I am elated' to have a use the individual in question must *be* saying it. What the above contrast then amounts to is essentially that between the speaker of the moment and the non-speaker. Thus if the contrast between selves and others is to yield an epistemological asymmetry at all, it must first yield an asymmetry within such a speaker and hearer situation.

At another level it might be said that anyway the question 'How do I know that I'm x?' must itself be spoken so that it too must pass muster in the light of the, let us say, earlier question, 'Why should I (anyone) say (ask) that?' But it is perhaps not yet clear why our question should take the form of a query as to purpose, motive, intent, or function. I want to try to make this clear and also to expand on the guide lines which first-personal utterances, *qua* utterances, must follow.

Before I do so something should be said to the critic who might say: The first person idiom may be restricted to the user of the 'medium of communication' but this medium need not be speech and perhaps such use need not even be communicated since expressions of first-personal form need not necessarily be uttered, they may, for instance, merely be thought. I could think that I'm elated and not have to say it. Without going into the relation between thought and speech this point could be readily surrendered. We are now interested in the context which produces the paradox of 'privileged first-person access'; this paradox cannot be stated without *some* form of presumed interchange between a speaker and a hearer; it is always the *parity* of the interchange which is sceptically questioned, isn't it? And, although this interchange need not be by means of speech, that particular form will do as well as any. The question before me is the question of whether a reversal of roles between a speaker and hearer in any way affects a change in the content, let us say, of those roles for the subsequent speaker or the previous hearer. If thinking does *not* provide a basis of such interchange then it is irrelevant here even though it might be true that not all first-personal utterances need be spoken or otherwise acted out. If, on the other hand, thinking does provide a basis for interchange between speaker and hearer then the differences between speaking and thinking are of no consequence to the issue. But now I want to return to the guide-lines which first personal utterances *qua* utterances must follow.

26. *Speech as action and its implications for the sceptic*

First, speech is action, and, if it needs adding, intentional action. Consequently an inquiry as to the purpose of such action will always be a fair question. Such purpose will needs go together with the fact that speech, as action, is a public undertaking. Obviously it is also more than merely public action since one of the general purposes for which we engage in speech is that it will be attended to in a way which involves a hearer *via* a speaker's use of certain conventions. Speech is then conventionalized action which involves another; it will be something we do intentionally to or for a hearer, and, since our speech action *is* conventionalized, the intent or point of the action will be available to the hearer in a way which goes with 'understand' rather than 'surmise'. For our purposes it is worth repeating that the function of a particular speech act must be construable both from the point of view of an act and an act which involves another – as hearer. The function or meaning or purpose of a speech act is then to be seen as conventionalized within its vocal public performance for a hearer.

This fact is supported by part of what we mean by 'convention': it is essentially a three-term affair with one term common to the other two. The common term in the case of speech is vocal-plus-gestural etc. action, and it must be available to both speaker and hearer in order to allow for agreement or ruling. When agreement is reached as to the function allowed a vocal action then both my use and your use of it will be understood, respectively, by the other. It is also of importance, if one of us is not to remain the only speaker, that the utterances, whose occurence is now to bear the agreed convention, be available for use by us both; thus the conventionalization of *vocal* action allows either of us to be speaker or hearer, although this allowance for change of roles would be obviously possible of any action serving as the conventionalized medium. Incidentally, vocal action also serves our need to tack our conventions to a type of occurrence which is difficult enough in performance not to occur inadvertently with too great a frequency but rather mostly requires us to some extent to try in order for it to happen. This is perhaps why when speech sounds occur we rarely, if ever, take them as mere inadvertent occurrences but as intentional in some fashion or other. Even a slip has import. Such import is available to the hearer, as is the import of other cases of displaced speech intention, only because, of course, of their construable relations to the primary intentions embodied in our non-displaced uses of speech.

Theories, then, which find an epistemological asymmetry between the first and the other persons – theories whose consequences we would therefore call sceptical – cannot, I think, be consistent with the aspects of speech mentioned above. The sceptic's theory as to what we might mean or intend by such an action as to say 'I am in pain' – an action loaded with conventionalized intent in the address of a hearer – makes it appear pointless that there should have been speech at all, that there should have occurred in*ten*tionally such an event at all. But that there should have occurred such an event is a presupposition of the sceptic's proposed asymmetry.

This may seem too quick a way against the sceptic. He can admit that whatever he says must purposely and purposefully involve the hearer; yet must he also admit that what he achieves in the saying may not serve a further, 'extra-linguistic' purpose, itself unsaid and unconventionalized, itself asymmetrically or privately known to him by means unavailable to us? I say to you, for example, that I'm in pain and the sceptic could admit it may be said to enlist your aid or your sympathy or to warn you, each in a way particular to some conventionalized or displaced use of the utterance. He could also agree that we differently cue our hearer with 'I have a fever', 'I'm cold', 'I have a bad itch', 'I'm in pain', 'My arm hurts', 'My tooth aches'. But the sceptic wants to add that in whichever fashion each of these utterances purposely and differently cues the hearer, the purpose, or part of the purpose, conventionally so to cue him has ultimately to do with my fever, my itch or my pain. What the hearer understands and expects as the result of my speech, how he responds, what the conventional interest contracted into the vocal performance may happen to be, all of these speaker-hearer covenants will be independent of the 'actual' intent associated with this expression only by me. My public speech acts, the sceptic must say, serve motives themselves not just contingently unconventionalized as part of speech but serve motives themselves unconventionaliz*able*. Within the range of cases under consideration, he says, it is as if there is to his speech a set of motives which are *systematically ulterior* to those vocal acts.

Now this issue is crucial for the personal asymmetrist, or sceptic, because his position cannot, within the terms he himself lays down, deny support to this particular point. If he is still to hold to some form of personal epistemological asymmetry the sceptic must, I think, now defend the notion of 'a systematically ulterior motive'. He is forced to this defence unless he wishes to deny that speech, as act, itself sets certain necessary limits to his position; but that there should be speech, within which the self-referential and other-referential contrast occurs, is necessary to his statement of the asymmetry.

Questions as to whether there can be a private language which were dealt with in the previous section need not I think deter us here as a possible block against the particular line I am now taking. They needn't because the sceptic is able, as I have already said, to formulate his personal paradoxes or personal asymmetries *only* with the presupposition that reports emanating from a source other than himself cannot be type-homogeneous with reports made by oneself. The sceptic's question is now a question of the parity of reports. The sceptic's problems about persons cannot, in short, be stated independently of the context of contrasted reports, or of a 'private' situation *in contrast* with an 'external' situation, or stated independently of the contrast of a first person *with* a second or third person situation. The possibility of such contrast or asymmetry rides upon the operability of some conventional form of interchange, in our case speech, between the persons. It is the interchange itself which must be said to function asymmetrically, i.e. sceptically. Without this interchange there could be no grounds for arguing for or against personal contrasts, no grounds for the sceptic's reservation as to the symmetries among speaker and hearer. And it is speech, a public language, which makes such symmetries seem apparent in the first place and hence provides the necessary presupposition against which the sceptic works, if he is to work at all.

Moreover it is only in speech, or something like it, that we find the distinction between speaker-restricted versus non-speaker-restricted devices – without which a sceptic's putative asymmetries epistemological or otherwise, could gain neither credence nor statement in the very first instance. It is for those reasons and surely others like them that the sceptical arguments must be prepared to face the implications which may be drawn from the use of speech. And it is this dependence of his scepticism upon speech and hence its intentional, conventional aspect which, I think, forces the sceptic to offer defence of the notion of systematically ulterior motives. These are the terms in which he can now be forced to argue if he is to project his sort of asymmetry among the three persons of speech.

27. *Systematically ulterior motives*

I should like consequently to examine the notion of a 'systematically ulterior motive' as it might be expected by a sceptic to work for him.

I tell you I feel depressed. Two not separate questions arise. Why should I tell this to *you* or to anyone? Why should I bother to *tell* at all? Well, I may tell *you* because you asked or you're sympathetic; there may, that is, be particular reasons why I select you to tell. But sometimes anyone might have done to tell. The point to emphasize is that whether or not we select our particular hearers promiscuously we must, if we tell, tell someone. 'Someone' is to whom things get told, if they are told. The fact that we necessarily involve someone else by the telling will have to figure in any account of what saying 'I feel depressed' is to mean.

But why, to turn to the second question, should I bother at all to tell that I feel depressed? Given that the particular person to whom I tell this may be more or less promiscuously selected can the saying or not saying of it also make no difference? It may, but it cannot always make no difference. Were it *always* the case that the performance of our particular speech actions were gratuitous, that anything we say might in those same circumstances have been left unsaid, and anything unsaid might in these same circumstances have been said, we should either be denying the possibility of adopting relevant speech conventions at all or denying the possibility of specifying singular enough circumstances to warrant any such action. In effect, this is the claim that to speak does not make a relevant difference, that, in effect, speech is not action.

Telling, I shall assume, is an action and may make a difference. And given that the telling is intentional, the difference, whatever it may be, afforded by the telling that I'm depressed, will be the purpose or intent or point of the thing.

Can the purpose of my saying that I'm depressed be merely because it is so? I think this is an incoherent possibility unless the unadorned *mere* fact of what is so can itself serve as a purpose for action which involves another. Too many things are so and too few things said, however, for this to be an answer. If we say things *merely* because they are so we don't yet know how to converse; unless, that is, systematic irrelevance is no barrier to the operations of speech. But among all the things that are so and that I know are so why should I have selected that I am depressed for the saying? Or, why not have selected something to say which is not so? Is it because I was not depressed a moment ago, or that now it is so acute all else is excluded? But why *say* anything at all? Why act in *this* way? Why should I not have hyperventilated yoga-fashion or taken a pill or a sweet – why the saying among all the other things I might have done?

I take it then that to have said something is to have meant to and consequently to make fair the question of what intent was served by the utterance; and to bring forward again our first question, it will have to be shown how this purpose could have been served or affected by the involvement of another, namely the hearer, for that too is the sort of action saying is. With this understood, I say 'I feel depressed'.

The sceptic argues for the possibility of his speech action's relation to a systematically ulterior motive; he argues for the possibility that the utterance has an aspect to its 'meaning' which it is said is 'private in principle', or at least not part of its conventionalizable use. This is to say that part of the reason for my having spoken at all is something to which only I can be privy; part of my purpose in having spoken at all is systematically unrelated to the act itself; (and were it not systematically unrelatable it would be relatable perhaps in the way many displaced senses come to be related to an earlier sense of an expression).

Now, I can get you to buy a longer car perhaps because of your oedipal insecurity, but that is not the dictionary meaning of 'longer car'; it is perhaps its displaced meaning, or an association. As a salesman, I might tell you that this car was longer than that one with the ulterior motive of triggering your oedipal mechanism. But this sort of case is obviously not the case before us. If you ask the sceptical protagonist what his systematically ulterior motive might be in saying he feels depressed, he can only reply, 'to tell you how I *feel*'. The salesman, though less honest, *could* be more articulate, indeed he himself was probably briefed in just what his ulterior motives were to be.

Could then *any* interest or purpose be served by the utterance that he feels depressed such that it will satisfy the asymmetrist; or such that we need worry about special 'senses' for speakers as opposed to hearers? I think not. For if we force the sceptic to accept as a pre-condition to the formation of his difficulties that they must have occurred as the result of the sort of action which is speech then, obviously, there could have been no reason to *act* in the very manner we must have acted for the precondition of the difficulties.

Why have acted or spoken at all unless what you hope to achieve by the action is serviceable in the domain of such action? Or, rather, there can be no aspect of your speech which can be both purposeful and systematically special to the speaker in its purpose. To have spoken is clearly to have been purposeful; but if one's motives are systematically ulterior to one's behaviour that behaviour certainly cannot have been purposeful.

28. *The sceptical position denies its own presuppositions*

Why have acted at all? Why have acted in a way which necessarily involves another? The sense in which we are left without answer to these questions is the sense in which it would have been pointless to have spoken on the sceptic's account; but that there should have been pointed speech in the first place is a *pre*-supposition of the entire business.

There are other threads here. If it is established that you had a motive it must also be establishable what that motive was. This is like saying that if it is on a particular occasion established that there is an affirmative answer to the question 'Did you (choose to) do that?', then the question 'Why did you (choose to) do that?' will also be answerable. Purposes, motives, intents are specifiable.

'Why did you (choose to) say you were depressed?' What was the point in your having so acted? It is established in the commission of the act itself that you had a motive; yet the sceptic must insist that his intents in the act of speech are systematically unspecifiable; then such 'speech' must be systematically unperformable.

In addition, the sceptic must employ, and yet deny the possible employment of, the speech presupposition of, *qua* speaker, involving another as hearer. The hearer's function becomes pre-empted when the sceptic claims special speaker-restricted means or special 'evidence' as operative in the commission of a first person utterance. But to pre-empt the hearer at *any* stage is to deny a necessary condition of the framing of the situation itself: it is the unsatisfactory asymmetry as *between* the first and second or third person, that is, the asymmetry between a speaker *and* a hearer or another, which is the basis of the sceptic's reaction. If we were to clean up the sceptic's position in relation to this point we should have to say something like the following. 'The speaker acts in a certain way but since he cannot ever produce reasons for having acted toward or spoken to any particular hearer he cannot specify upon whom he so "acts". If we cannot say that the speaker speaks to the hearer, i.e. acts intentionally in relation to a particular hearer, then we cannot later be sceptical concerning this "unperformed action's" effect upon a "hearer" who was never its intended locus anyway.'

VI. Epistemology (B)

What is the upshot of all this? First, it seems we must accept the unexceptionable principle that before I can answer how I know that I'm x, I must know why I *say* that I'm x. Hence, any reason I may have for so saying cannot be systematically denied my hearer and still be an aspect of the meaning, purpose, function or intention of my speech act. Reasons so restricted could only be systematically ulterior to any speech act of mine, i.e. unrelatable to it.

If we grant the guiding question before us is 'Why should I *say* I am x?' then commerce with a hearer is presupposed. Such commerce further implies that our speeches must be actions which any speaker would be equally capable of performing. The limitations upon who may be the speaker are contingent. Where there are only contingent restrictions as regards interchange of roles between first and second person it cannot be the nature of these roles, or of the actions which constitute these roles, that they contain non-transferable functions, purposes, intentions *or* criteria.

Suppose we accept the question 'Why should I *say* that I'm x' as a working guide to how we are to proceed with the troublesome asymmetry inherent in the question of how I know that I'm x. This means we have accepted that there cannot be a sceptical answer to that question; but it need not commit us to accepting the question itself as *bona fide*. With an eye to this last contingency let us look at some of the conceivable answers to, 'How does one know that one is x?' where 'x' could be what has been resignedly called a mental state or consciousness predicate.

29. *Unhelpful answers to 'How do you know you are x?'*

(a) Clearly it will be of no help to answer that 'being x' or 'the fact that I *am* x' is how I know that I'm x. 'How do you know the tit is bearded?' is not satisfactorily answered by 'It is bearded'; and 'How do you know you're testy?' is not, except testily, answered by, 'because I'm testy'. To question how you are in a position to know something is not to ask what it is that you claim to know; that information is already part of the questioning utterance itself. 'How do you know . . .?' is, roughly, a question of your credentials for a claim perhaps made at an earlier time; it is in any case not correct merely to repeat a claim whose licence is being legitimately solicited. And, of course, 'How do you know?' may not *always* be a legitimate solicitation.

(b) Nor will it, I think, help to reply some such thing as, 'I feel it', even where feeling may seem to be appropriate matter. To, 'How do you know you're giddy, or hurting, or depressed?', 'I feel giddy', etc., is no answer. The question would not have been much changed in the first instance were we to have asked, 'How do you know you feel giddy?' It is presupposed that giddiness, depression, pain, etc. will be *felt*. Thus I may not produce 'I feel it' as a credential since it is itself contained within the claim which is being questioned. To give such an answer would be either like merely repeating the claim when its credibility is questioned or like suggesting that I might have a sensation or feeling or mental state without feeling it. But again, these answers may not help here because nothing could.

On the other hand there are circumstances involving material objects under which it is helpful, when asked how one knows that such and such is the case, to reply, that one hears, or sees, or is touching, or tasting, or smelling, or has been told it. These replies are individually helpful because there are usually *other* possible sense-means by which we might have come to know. Thus the particular means by which we have actually come to know will be helpful in the assessment of the claim. It is when there can in the nature of the case be *no* other means by which we might have come better to know that the reply is unhelpful. Isn't this partly why, 'How do you know you're in pain?' resembles, 'How do you know there is red in your visual field?' or, 'What makes you say you hear a scraping-like sound?' or, 'How do you know it feels smooth to you?' or, 'How do you know it tastes salty to you?' It is strange in these cases to ask for credentials not just because 'looks', 'sounds', 'feels', 'tastes', are signs of 'weakened' claims. In each case there is no other credential we could possibly offer than what is already implicit in the claim. These are already the strongest reasons we could have. We do not know how it looks to us other than by having seen; how it sounds to us other than by having heard; how it hurts us other than by feeling. In this sense 'How do you know you're in pain?' is a query about something the singular presuppositions of which would answer the question; it consequently has no answer except to point out what has been ignored.

It may then be a property of a certain class of claims that there are to the claimant no other means at present available than those already incorporate to the claim which could serve as a means to cross-check them; and often no means are available by which to re-check them. In such circumstances it is fruitless to ask for underwriting or assurance or how it is known for we know the answers and their limits before we ask. The claim itself already contains the means by which we have come to know. And, of course, the means themselves would not be questionable in the same way.

30. *Feeling*

We can be certain that 'How do you know that you are x?' does not have a solipsistic or sceptical answer because of the relationship of this query to 'claiming' or 'saying'. But even if we go on to grant that this epistemological query, as it is applied to *certain* states, emotions, sensations, etc., is to be discounted for the reasons just given, we are still left with the problem of providing a non-sceptical account of 'feeling'. The sceptic might still say, 'Granted, the epistemological query is odd. But its oddness, though not now based on the assumption that we 'know' x-sorts of things in ways we do not know other sorts of things nevertheless assumes that we do *feel* x-sorts of things. And feelings, we are told again, are private in a way other aspects of our knowledge are not; our feelings are our own and about us in a way our other knowledge is not. I want to examine the ways in which our feeling x may be said to differ from other claims of ours. Three topics of comparison will be used: 31. Tactual and Non-Tactual Feelings; 32. Non-Tactual Feelings and the Other Senses; 33. Corrigibility.

31. *Tactual and non-tactual feelings*

There is a close connexion, I think, between feeling pain, or depressed, or giddy, or edgy, and what we might call tactual feeling. Feeling a pain in one's finger does not differ significantly in grammar or physiology from the feel of the texture or the pressure of the pen in one's hand. It may be that we do develop tactual skills but that we do not develop skill at feeling giddy – although some people are better than others, say, at discerning displaced pains. There are anyway certain tactual sensations which are not any more the result of skills than are sensations of this or that state of one's own. The pressure of the pen or, within limits, the feel of certain textures would be examples. The main difference that need concern us at this point between a tactual or 'outer' feeling and a non-tactual feeling is that instances of the former may involve feeling external objects, or parts of ourselves, while inner feelings are limited by definition to ourselves. This may contribute to the difference in skills between tactual and non-tactual feelings. Information and discriminations about objects which are common between speaker and hearer are more consistently useful than information and discriminations about ourselves. This *may* contribute to the difference but what surely does contribute is the local difference in nerve endings between our inner organs and our hands, say. Otherwise why not say either: Tactual and non-tactual feelings are the same sensuous mode, or admit there is a sixth sense.

32. *Non-tactual feelings and the other senses*

This difference of nerve endings does not mark the feeling in one's stomach or head as less comparable to the feelings in our fingers than to such feelings as we have on the skin in the middle of our back. The fact that I may with my hands feel things other than myself but not do so with my liver seems more distinctive. It is, however, clearly not a fact. For whatever I may feel with my fingers I may, though less plainly, feel with my liver. The sensations I get in my fingers or my liver as they come in contact with things are useful as information perhaps about those things. Feelings I get in my fingers or liver when they are not in contact with objects other than themselves are useful as information about me, another object.

There is yet no reason for taking 'inner feelings as more or less private or in any distinctive way different from 'outer' feelings. If my stomach is probed with an instrument of gastro-intestinal exploration, is that feeling more private or less public than those I have as I wash my hands or grip the bat? You may grip the bat. And of course you too may have your stomach probed. But what of cases where there is no 'external' cause or object involved in the feeling? Isn't the claim that 'inner' feelings are different than at least some 'outer' feelings dependent upon the fact that we may somehow relate our 'outer' feelings with other sensual modes. The bat handle may both feel and look smooth, or feel and sound hard. But the probing instrument too may feel and also look hard or rough. Thus the important distinction, it could be argued, is not *where* we feel what we feel, whether in our hands or our head, but whether these feelings are connected with some dissociable material particular or not. It is on these grounds perhaps that the publicity or lack of it, or other asymmetry of non-tactual feeling as a sense of mode, is made out.

This won't do either, of course, since a paradigm case of a private feeling is a pain independent of whether it has a purely organic, 'internal' source or is produced by 'external' means.

It seems to me, to generalize on this present lack of difference between tactual and non-tactual feelings, that any sense in which a non-tactual feeling may be said to be non-public is that in which any sensuous mode may be said to be so. For instance, tastes, sounds, glimpses, no less than tactual feels and non-tactual feels, are private in the strict sense that these already-particular sensations may, if we are to have rules of identity, be had by no other than the senser. On the other hand, the sense in which such sensations *may* be had or shared by others, if we are to have rules of similarity, can be duplicated for our non-tactual feelings as well.

The view I am supporting is that there are few differences, and these only contingent, between our tactual and non-tactual feelings. These contingent differences are not enough to support the 'privacy' needed by the sceptic for non-tactual feeling without, for lack of difference, including all our sense modalities under this cloak. But he cannot do this and hope for the contrast he needs between 'privacy' and 'non-privacy'. Should his argument be that all our sensual information is equally deserving of the sceptical distrust of privacy, he is on the road to solipsism. To stay off it he needs to recognize some safe ground, and if he does then all ground is safe for there is no difference of ground.

The sceptic might however make the more interesting claim that our non-tactual feeling is asymmetrically placed among the other senses because such feeling alone among other apprehensions may not be cross-checked with our other senses. I cannot see or hear or taste a headache; but I can feel and see a surface, or I can feel it even while you see it. There is on the other hand only one means of sensing a headache. This won't do either.

First, because some sense modes, or perhaps all, do not go together with other sense modes any better than they do with non-tactual feelings: a colour perception, for example. I cannot feel or taste or hear a colour; nor can I taste or see or smell a sound.

The second reason we cannot separate off our non-tactual feelings on the grounds that they are private in the sense that they are not supportable or checkable by other sense means is that the ways in which such cross-reference does seem possible with our other senses is precisely duplicable for the non-tactual feeling cases. This is a crucial point since, if it is true, then our non-tactual feelings will be in no more a unique position as regards our other senses than is any other single sense in relation to the others; but should this duplication of other sense-support not be possible for 'internal' feelings then it will, I think, not be possible for any other single sense.

For example then, what I see I may also touch without of course touching in any sense being seeing, as it were. In this strict sense, of course, *what* I actually experience as I see I do not experience as I touch, unless I want to say that I feel or touch shade and light. What I do is touch or feel *where* the shadow or the light falls. Similarly if I hear the clock ticking I may see that it ticks but not see the tick, as it were. If there are *any*, correlations let us say, among the senses then these would be cases. And these cases are duplicable for non-tactual feelings.

If I feel giddy it may be seen that I am giddy – by me or by others – and sometimes heard or sniffed. If I am in pain that may be seen or heard. Of course what I hear or see is not the feeling; but neither did I see the sound of the clock. Should we find it possible to deny that feeling giddy may be supported by seeing or hearing that one is giddy then we should have to deny that there are correlations possible among *any* of the senses: to see is not to hear is not to touch is not to smell is not to taste, is not to feel.

But connexions among the senses are possible. And the connexions between non-tactual feeling and some of the other senses is no less distant or hypothetical or weak or conjectural than any other sense and the rest.

What is true, however, is that some senses are fitted to certain kinds of observations while others then come in in their own way in a secondary or supportive role; at least to begin with. Thus, that depression or giddiness or pain are felt is as uninformative as the fact that colour is seen, or sound is heard or pressure is felt. There are no better ways for these things to come to us although we do learn to relate these best ways with other supportive ways. Hence, I can see the nearby clock must be not merely running but ticking were it not encased in a vacuum; and I can see that he must still be in pain were it not that he is drugged, etc.[1]

As we might have suspected there will be cases, such as the ascription of textures, where two senses are of more nearly equal weight. The nap may look soft or feel soft. Better cases are found among smells and tastes. If we notice a smell or taste, say of garlic, either sense would serve independently of the other, and neither sense need be secondary here as in the afore-mentioned case where, in judging softness, sight would take second place to touch. The point to remember is that there are cases, not limited to non-tactual feelings alone, where a particular sort of ascription may depend primarily and fully upon one sense and only secondarily upon others. But this yields us no grounds for isolating that particular perception such that it must be sceptically suspect. What it does mean is that some forms of perception, including non-tactual feelings, go with observations to which they are best and sufficiently, *and in a sense, exclusively, suited.*

What also may often come to pass is that observations fitted

[1] A suggestion which intrudes here but which will be amplified later is: discard behaviourism, the view that certain senses or feelings don't exist, and work instead on how the various senses, *including* non-tactical feelings, may be correlated with each other. The fiction that sight is the only sense may be transplanted by the truth that sight is our most dominant and fruitful sense.

in the past to one particular sense, such as in the case of feeling giddy, may subsequently become supportable by, or cross-referred with, observations fitted to another sometimes superior sense such as sight. You might, for instance, have a physio-chemical account of my giddiness or tiredness. There will be no reason why 'felt giddiness' cannot give way in the direction of the superior sense of sight to 'seen giddiness'. This is possible even though the ways in which seeing is superior to feeling – measurability, for instance – are contingent and even though seeing that I'm tired must initially have been only supportive of and derivative from feeling that I'm tired: this hinges upon the way in which feelings are literally not seeable. But seeing that I'm tired will remain merely supportive of feeling that I'm tired only so long as our notion of tiredness retains its old allegiance to the sense of feeling; but there is no reason why this allegiance *must* be preserved. There is no reason why 'tiredness' (not the feeling) may not become a purely visual concept.

I think this leaves us with the following parallel. You say you feel x, and though the challenge of how you can know this is now seen as unimportant, there is a question as to how I may know this of you without sceptical implications. After all, *you* feel x and I do not; and neither my observations of you nor my feeling x under similar circumstances will be quite like your evidence that you do, or so it is said. In parallel with this you say for instance that the lime tastes bitterly, or rather that the lime tastes bitterly to you. There is then a question as to how I may know this of you without sceptical implications. After all, *you* taste the bitter and I do not; and neither my observations of you nor my tasting the lime as bitter under similar circumstances will be quite like your evidence that you do. But my tasting the lime as bitter under similar enough circumstances will be evidence as good as we need ever get that it tasted bitterly to you – short of our being you. To ask for more evidence or to hold off your taste of the bitter as unapproachable is only to take refuge in the law of identity; it would be to insist that circumstances could never be sufficiently similar for me to be you. But of course, they needn't be. Anyway, if one perseveres in the view that circumstances may never be sufficiently similar for me to check on an observation of yours, then the issue is the simpler case of solipsism, or systematically private language.

But what of the case of your feeling x? How does the parallel go? I think it can in principle go all the way. The difference is the contingent one of greater complexity in duplicating conditions for the case of feeling x. To be reasonably certain that we have available sufficiently similar circumstances for me to check on an observation of yours in the case of taste we need consider only such obvious things as similar taste apparatus, previous agreement in other cases of bitterness, or perhaps other tastes, previous agreement on the use of the word 'taste', no intervening tastes or other such possible dullers of the taste buds, agreement that the same lime or same part are involved and so on. To require 'previous agreement' is not, I think, to beg the question but only to insist we start this side of systematically private language. Should, however, this move toward availability of sufficiently similar circumstances be one of actually begging the question against the *im*possibility of my feeling just what you feel in the same sense as I can have seen just what you have seen then this is just what we want to do – beg the question against a view which leads to incoherence. Availing ourselves then of the possibility of sufficiently duplicating your conditions for my own case I could in principle tell whether it tasted bitterly to you or not. In the same way, I think, it is possible in principle to duplicate conditions for myself such that I can tell whether, under these conditions, you did feel x or not. It will be more complex, as I say, and in some cases impracticable as when you report a rather particular thing angers or depresses you. To check this I myself should need to sufficiently duplicate your past, but never follow the solecism of 'identically' duplicating it. And for most cases our pasts are already similar enough – so that only minor adjustments would be needed to sufficiently duplicate the conditions under which your, claim let us say, is made. That such sufficient similarity is possible and present is of course the premise upon which our teaching of the names of these experiences is based. It is also a premise of much of science, and, as I hope to argue, a premise of coherence in these matters.

More particularly, if you claim you are angry and I wish to check this as closely as possible, I may duplicate your chemical, physiological, and related psychological states and see whether I am angry under your conditions. This is just as when you claim to see Venus through the glass I check by duplicating as far as is necessary your conditions of making the claim: I step up to the glass. And I have more than enough assurance as to the sufficient similarity of the other relevant conditions involved.

These sorts of ways are as close as we need get to checking on an utterance of another without doing the impossible, that is, without being him. *But this is a general truth for all classes of utterance whether they are of oneself or of external things, whether of states of consciousness or physical objects.* And if we are satisfied with such possible checks in the case of some physical object statements then we must be satisfied with them in the case of purely personal utterances. If we are dissatisfied with such checks in either case then we must be dissatisfied in both cases, in which event we are without *any* checks and back at the more tractable case of SPL.

This by the way may account for one way in which sight is superior to feeling for some of our purposes: it is a much simpler matter to produce sufficiently similar conditions for me to check upon visual claims than to check certain of your feeling claims.

It perhaps needn't be added that under normal conditions we needn't go so far as to duplicate for ourselves the conditions under which another makes a first-person statement with himself as topic or even something else as topic. Where circumstances are usual we accept secondary checks such as our observations or the conditions of his statement itself. That we have access, however, to the extreme sort of checks I have outlined is important as backing both for our normal trust in our other-ascriptions as well as our understanding of the self-ascriptions of others. It is also important that these extreme checks which involve us in reproduction of sufficiently similar conditions are seen not only as the limit of what is attainable but as sufficient in reason. Two things the sceptic insists upon which *are* the far side of the attainable are, first, that conditions cannot be sufficient until they are identical rather than similar. But the expectation or insistence that I must be you before I may experience what you have has self-defeating consequences. The second thing insisted upon by the sceptic was that his feeling x cannot ever be satisfactorily checked by me should I use in the check another sense, such as sight. There is a way in which this is true but it is then true of any sense in respect of any other (except perhaps some cases of taste and smell). No sight ever supports the statement that I have heard a sound the *way* the hearing of the sound itself would, or the way the hearing of the sound again would, etc. This sort of matter will be discussed in the section on corrigibility to follow. Thus if the sceptic's requirement is that I must, in order to be able to non-sceptically ascribe feelings of x to you, feel what you have felt, must, that is, be able to use the same sense as it were, then this condition can be met, granted that sufficiently similar circumstances are available. And if they are not in principle available the consequent argument that I may not feel what you feel collapses of its own weight in the way the notion of systematically private language did.

33. *Corrigibility*

I take a first distinction between corrigible and incorrigible statements to be as follows. Incorrigible statements are those made upon such basis that either the adduction or subduction of *other* means of support is irrelevant to the truth of the statement. The truth of corrigible statements, on the other hand, is affected by the addition or subtraction of *other* means of support than that first made use of. Statements as to our personal feelings of the x-variety are thought to be incorrigible in that no other evidence presented either to me or open to you could gainsay the fact that I do feel pain or feel depressed or exhilarated or queezy. This is not in conflict with the truth that the absence of certain normally correlated behaviour of mine might lead you to doubt, less or more, that I did so feel.

There are at least two aspects to this attempt to make a place of difference for our feelings in respect of our other sense media. First there is the obvious case already discussed that no other sense can serve as anything but supportive of statements about our feelings; for a class of cases 'I feel it' is supreme as a means of evidence and, if true, cannot be countermanded by any other means. Second, there is the possible point that there is no distinction either available or needed between an imaginary and a real pain, *qua* pain. In both cases the pain is actually felt though the causes differ. But the fact that evidence other than feeling is irrelevant to certain claims is without implication as to the epistemological asymmetry of our feelings in respect of the other senses. Any of the other senses as we have seen is supreme to a certain class of statements in the same way that 'I feel it' is supreme to a class of its own. But these are, even taken all together, a rather limited and highly inutile class of utterance which we might call 'singly sense-oriented'. It is their limited function which makes them incorrigible in respect of any other evidence than the sense to which they are expressly tailored. They would be such notorious claims as 'I feel giddy', 'I hear a buzzing', 'I smell a smell like that of mock orange', 'I see blue', 'I have a sour taste (in my mouth)', and so on. There is a corresponding set of utterances which are not singly sense-oriented but rather object-oriented sense statements. 'I feel the feather', 'I hear the train', 'I smell the mock orange', etc. would be the obvious examples of a class which makes first person present indicative use of a sensual verb which takes a material object term, or a strong implication of that, as object.

For every object-oriented sense statement there exists at least one related singly sense-oriented statement. If you tell me that you smell the mock-orange you may be asked how it smells to you and you may reply that it smells pungently. If I ask you how you know that it is the mock-orange you smell you may answer in a variety of ways, described by John Austin in Other Minds, which either give evidence as to your familiarity with the particular scent of mock-orange or support your olefactory evidence with other sense evidence such as visual, etc.

But if you tell me you smell a pungent odour we have seen the inutility of asking how you know that you do. Singly sense-oriented statements can have no better evidence than the sensual material they already claim. Certainly no other sensual mode could countermand a singly sense-oriented claim. What could you see (or touch or hear) that would make you think you were not smelling a pungent odour? (Let it be for now given that you are careful and know what a pungent odour is.) Is it that the room was full of roses? But the claim was not about how roses smell and it was not about what you thought you smelled or what you seemed to smell or what it was as if you had smelled. These would all be sense-oriented *object* claims and not singly sense-oriented claims. How does it feel to you? or How does it smell to you? are questions which call for singly sense-oriented judgments without other commitment. And of course such sense-oriented claims may be made with or without the implied presence of material objects. They may be made in contexts of hallucination or illusion or sensual malfunction; or even more likely in contexts where we may try to unstructure and put into disparate sensual terms what may also be put otherwise.

It seems to me that in cases where we ascribe, say in the indicative mood, a property to a physical object, there are at least two, let us say presuppositions, invoked. If I tell you, not on hearsay, that the facing on the Buchanan Building is blue, you have a right at least to suppose first, that my optical apparatus is in normal, not abnormal, condition; second that external conditions of viewing are normal and usual for such purposes. And I may fault you on what you have told me when either of these presuppositions turn out to have been even unintentionally violated. Should, for instance, the first of these not be the case I could perhaps claim that you had had an hallucination or, if the second, that you had been the victim of an illusion. And there will be appropriate ways of saying this – 'The facing on the Buchanan Building isn't blue, you thought it was', or 'There's no such building', or 'It only looks (from here) as if it's blue'.

What I am suggesting then is that it is possible although as I have said, highly inutile – and this may account for our discomfort with the artificiality of most such examples put forward – to make utterances *without* such presuppositions as above and hence not to be open to fault in those ways. Of course the tendency is for there to be few, if any, such unpresuppositioned utterances in the language since they allow the hearer a minimum of information and prediction: they give us no ready clues as to the *conditions* of the utterance.

Well, 'What colour do you see now?'; 'I see red'. This exchange may be given a context, say of optometrist and patient, such that the reply seems of an incorrigible status in that no evidence may be brought forward to countermand it, since it attempts neutrality with respect to our normal presupposition which operate in cases where we ascribe 'a property to an object'. And because of the insularity of these particular sensual claims they are also not susceptible to the counter-evidence of other senses. 'This can't be a feeling like that of roughness I'm having because what I am touching looks smooth', is an incoherence. Nor, if it feels rough, *need* it be rough.

If we should grant the apparent isolation of an unpresuppositioned singly sense-oriented claim in what sense then may they be said to be incorrigible? If a claim limits itself not only to a single sense mode but also to a report of only that particular kind of unpresuppositioned sensuous information then it seems to provide no basis for correction either by other senses or for failure to conform to normal etc. conditions. I want to produce a reminder however which shows that even should this be true such a claim would still have been made on a basis which allows for possible checks as to its truth, and hence its untruth.

You claim that something feels rough to you or that you are in pain. Now should you actually and alone feel roughness or feel pain then nothing, as we have seen, could gainsay that. But should we be doubtful of your veracity or competence then we do have means with which to check upon the truth or veridicality of the claim. Sufficiently similar conditions would allow us to do that; and the rejection of their sufficiency could only be contingent unless 'different' is to mean, irrelevantly, 'another individual'. When the sufficiently similar conditions require changes in normal perceptual apparatus or quite special intervening conditions we may say that the claim was hallucinatory or illusory or otherwise the result of special conditions but we do not say it was false if the claim made no pretence as to the normality or non-speciality of the conditions. Should the claim be, for instance, that the rug was rough it would have been judged false the moment we discovered the conditions and apparatus of observations were abnormally aberrant. Such claims as the last contain a presupposition of normal conditions and apparatus of observation. But claims of the sort in question commit themselves to no such presupposition and hence are judged veridical or otherwise on their own conditions; and even they may be so judged since the conditions are *available* to judgment. Should we sufficiently duplicate conditions and discover no such experience as claimed we should be in a position either to accuse the claimant of deceit, or incompetence with the language, let us say.

The upshot of this is that we find incorrigibility to be the property not of any particular form of experience but of a rather limited set of utterances fitted however to all sense modes. The singular sense-orientation of these claims places them in no competition with other sense modes and contains no presupposition as to general or usual or standard conditions of observation, but limits itself to those of the particular situation *whatever* they may be. Without these two variables there is indeed no room for normal error since the situation is required to conform with only what it itself is. But this does not mean that we may not check upon such claims by sufficiently reproducing their conditions. Thus what we have in the incorrigibility of x-claims is a *general* feature found among all sense claims of a singly sense oriented sort. This removes the grounds for any asymmetry of function among x-claims as well as grounds for asymmetrical scepticism as to the checkability of such incorrigible claims.

What are we to say then when we find ourselves still tempted by the sceptically-minded principle that I cannot have the basis for saying that Enos is in pain that Enos may have in saying that he is? The most persuasive move is to extend the implications which go along with the denial of sense to: 'I can have the same basis for saying of him that he is in pain that he has for saying so of himself'. The implications of a denial of sense to this are extended as follows.

Lack of satisfaction with the production of 'sufficiently similar circumstances' which fill the epistemological gap between me and you would lead, in consistency, to lack of acceptance not only in the sort of case before us where mental states are involved but also in the case of *any* ascription involving even material objects: I cannot have the basis for saying that the shoe shines that Enos has for saying this. If we accept this move then we have no sceptical contrast between self-ascription and other-ascription, no way of containing the sceptic's case, since every ascription now seems to have an overly-personal basis. As I have already argued, this is the easy case of either solipsism or systematically private language. If on the other hand we do not reject the role of 'sufficiently similar circumstances' then I may have precisely the same basis for saying that Enos is in pain that Enos may have in saying that he is. 'Meaning and criteria' need not differ. It is no longer a matter of my placing trust in a different form of evidence than does he – as, for instance, the trust of my mere observations of him as opposed to his trust of his actual experience; it is only a contingent convenience which so limits me. We may, when the situation calls for it, both undergo the actual and qualitatively identical experience.

I want now to put some of these arguments to further and related use on the purported distinction between personal self-ascription and material self-ascription.

VII. Self-ascription and other Ascription

34. *Material self-ascription and personal self-ascription*

We have seen earlier, in Chapter I, that it is too transparent to argue that *all* cases of self-ascription will be asymmetrical to other-ascriptions. This would be the case of the too-lonely 'I'. It is consequently a corollary to the position which holds there is something substantive to first-person asymmetry that it be limited to a sub-class of self-ascriptions. Unless the game is to be up at once there must be at least something I have in common with others. Plurals are necessary. Hence it is held that only a *sub*-class of self-ascriptions differs from material body ascriptions in a type-distinct way. The remainder of the class of self-ascriptions is part of the larger class of material body ascriptions. In this way it has been claimed there are Minds and Bodies, my body in a class with others; or there are P-properties, or Psychical properties, and M-properties, my Material properties in a class with others.

(If the distinction between M- and P-predicates is taken radically enough to imply that individuating principles of a type-distinct sort are required to support that predicate difference, then my earlier contention, in Chapter III, that there is a type-homogeneity between our personal and impersonal demonstratives will be some explanation of why a *reductio* is possible of a view which insists that our personal predicates are subject to type-distinct difficulties not inherent among our uses of the impersonal predicates.)

I want to argue two things related to this traditional type-separation of certain personal and impersonal predicates. First, that self-ascriptive P-utterances are not a better ground for scepticism, not more problematic, than are first person M-utterances. I want to argue that there are conditions under which P-utterances are person-neutral just as there are conditions under which one material object may without scepticism be substituted for another, say, in an experiment. Hence, if the traditional type-separation of predicates depends upon the sceptical fertility of one class as opposed to the other, then such dependence will have been removed. I begin this first point by looking negatively at two tests which have in the past, I think, directed predicates into either the M- or the P-camps.

Second, I try to suggest *why* we should in the past have been tempted to hold that somehow first-person P-utterances are different from other-person P-utterances in a way we were untempted to hold that M-utterances are different across that same shift-in-person case.

Suppose we being with two lists each containing representatives of the two sorts of predicate. First, a list of P-predications which are said to apply to one's state of consciousness, moods, sensations, memories and so on and also a list of M-predications which are said to apply to the state, position and other descriptions of one's body. Some items will seem closer to those of the other list than are others: but my case will be made equally in terms of the staunchest member of each list.

P-Predication	*M-Predication*
I am coming.	I am freckled.
I am giddy.	I am heavy.
I am hurting.	I am short.
I am hoping . . .	I am at the delicatessen.
I am remembering . . .	I am six foot tall.

As far as I can make out there are two main tests which are meant to direct candidates into one or other of these lists. There is, I think, a third, but hidden, test: paradox. This test, which is meant to mark P-predicates, will actually be my main topic as we progress. First then, there is the non-transferability of P-predicates but apparently not of M-predicates. Second, there is a supposed shift in the 'quality' of a P-ascription as we change from a first-person to, say, a second-person association. Thus my giddiness has to me a quality, it is claimed, which it does not have for you; nor yours for me. But in whichever way my giddiness appears to you it may also appear to me. Among M-ascriptions however, there is, so it goes, no change in meaning or quality to the predicate as we shift it from the first to the other persons. This is in parallel with the absence of change in the 'meaning' of *any* external material body predicate although its ascriber may be said to change. Such 'physical' or M-ascriptions are speaker-neutral.

It is worth a diversion to note that when the reference is held constant in the expression, 'The noodles are mouldy', when used by different speakers about the same situation, there is no raising of the question as to whether 'mouldy' is differently affected as different ascribers make the statement. Of course where there is the relevant sort of trouble with 'mouldy' there should be similar trouble with 'The noodles'. We shall have to be given reasons why there should be a difference between self- and other-ascription of a P-predicate and not also between my use of a particular M-predicate and your use of it. We shall also need to be assured that such a difference is coherent. This will be of importance in the sequel. I want to move now into the examination of the first of the two tests.

35. *Non-transferability*

P-predicates are said to be non-transferable in a way M-predicates are not. But even though there is something proprietary about my hope, my giddiness, etc., there is an identical proprietariness to my shortness, my position, or girth. Perhaps, however, my freckles or my cornea are transferable to you. Such transference is possible because of the part-whole relation such things have to our person. Parts in a sense are identifiable separately from their wholes and, consequently, logically transferable to other wholes. In the other cases listed, supposing the list to be a fair one, part-whole is not the operative relation. And where it is not, there is a sense in which one's heft or precise weight, one's position, or height, are non-transferable for they are particularized aspects of the body total and thus have no principle of identity apart from the body total.

Some members of the M-list may be transferable. But some are not. Hence non-transferability cannot be a sorting principle of predicates as between their M-ness or P-ness, what*ever* that may be.

In any case as we saw in section 6, the test of non-transferability merely clouds the issue which is, only by over-extension of a single case into metaphor, to be taken as one of 'possession', and hence possible exchange, of an attribute. The issue is more a matter of whether there are among predicates two different sorts of association with the first person demonstrative as we change from the M-group to the P-group. Are our states, intentions, memories and sensations identifiable in a way in which our bodily characteristics are not? If they are, then the first personal pronoun will be ambiguous as between these two lists; it is after all the identifying device in these cases. It is taken as evidence of there actually being operative *two* separate means of identification that my states, intentions, memories, sensations, once identified as mine, are then never in principle identifiable apart from that proprietary connexion. Since they are never identifiable as someone else's they are non-transferable, it is said. But this, as we saw, is as true of at least some members of the M-list – my height, my heft, my position. And it will not do to shift these into the P-list since they are paradigm cases of body predicates with too much in common with material object predicates. Should we manipulate the members of these lists on the principle of non-transferability versus transferability the distinction between M and P would become one merely of part-whole ascription *versus* non-part-whole ascription.

Non-transferability, as it occurs in both lists, is actually a function of the law of identity of some predicates. There is a class of predicates which comprises physical aspects or modes *as well as* sensations, etc., whose members are dependent for their identification or specification upon association with a total body or total part of that body. Such predicates are non-transferably identifiable. But this is a feature which is indiscriminate as regards any other differences among predicates – including their purported M-ness and P-ness. The reason certain bodily predicates are transferable, i.e., identifiable or associable with a new particular, is because they are parts, rather than aspects of bodies with a possible identity of their own and thus associable and identifiable with other particulars as we may choose. Parts, in effect, are sub-particulars. The only point of the non-transferability test is then to tell us that, once particularized, some predicates are and some are not capable of having their present particularity relocated. Particular aspects, once particular, are not so relocatable; particular parts, are.

36. *P-claims, M-claims and sufficiently similar circumstances*

The second test has a single form with many variations. For brevity, let P stand for any present tense indicative use of a P-predicate where it is also understood that the grammatical person of the utterance is indicated in subscript. 'Pi' ('I am P') would stand for a first person use and 'Py' ('You are P') for the predicate in its second person use. The same convention is to apply to M-predicates. The second test may then be stated as follows: In the move from Mi to My there is no question of a shift in meaning or criteria or quality of M as we change persons. In M-cases the rules of similarity and sameness of ascription are clear and they are not easily confused with the rules of identity of ascription. Either I am heavy or you are heavy or we are equally heavy; either I am at the grocer's or you are or we both are. And I may make such observations of you *as easily* and by the same means as you may of yourself. There is said to be no other change than that of speaker in the move from Mi to My: what is said of each speaker and how we know it is thought to be constant. M-ascriptions are speaker-neutral. Contrariwise, a shift from Pi to Py has been said to involve more than a change in ascriber. Pi ascriptions are not made on the same grounds as Py ascriptions, it is said. Pi observations are not of the same order as Py observations – hence, probably the term 'non-observations'.[1]

I want to challenge this second test by showing that this purported gap between Pi and Py utterances should, for reasons of parity, be found between Mi and My utterances. But it is not. For these same, now reciprocal reasons, the gap is not present in the former case. For convenience sake we may treat M-utterances as any material body ascription while the different sub-scripts will again indicate different grammatical persons.

In order to argue for the parallel behaviour of M- and P-utterances when a change in person occurs, suppose the following kind of case offered by John Wisdom. There are neighbouring houses, yours and mine; and we have never visited. I, from my house, hear what in my house are characteristic sounds of a tea party emanating from your house. Can I, on the strength of such 'symptoms' or 'evidence', say that you are having a tea party? And if I do can I satisfy the sceptic who may argue that this is based on either an unsatisfactory induction or analogy? Well, I don't have to rely on mere analogy: I could conceivably be invited to your next party: your house is not in principle closed to me. Neither, and for the same reason, need the induction be systematically unsatisfactory because of the unavailability of one of the terms. Always, in the last analysis, I may witness the tea party itself.

On the other hand, both induction and analogy seem unsatisfactory where your house is in principle closed to me – where I cannot, in principle, feel your pain.

Consequently, for P-cases to be allowed to behave as do M-cases, we must provide for a sense in which I may visit your house. We must provide for a sense in which I may actually undergo what you undergo rather than to be so systematically distanced from it that I may only 'argue' to it.

When you say there was a tea party at your house, My, then

[1] See G. E. M. Anscombe's *Intentions*, Blackwells, 1957.

I may make the *same* claim, Mi, that there was a tea party at your house. We are assured that 'M' is not, ambiguous let us say, as between our claims so long as conditions were sufficiently similar for their making. I could sit close enough to where you sit, see what you see, hear what you hear. And all of these identities are themselves underwritten by the fact that sufficiently similar conditions inhere between us so that what we hear and see are sufficiently similar. Otherwise we are in the position of affirming that – let us put it the strong way – identical conditions could produce different results.

This background possibility of sufficiently similar circumstances makes my M-utterance capable of achievement on grounds sufficiently similar to those of your M-utterance such that there is no gap between Mi and My. This claim is speaker-neutral. Whatever gap there is, is not one between our claims but is that of our non-identity. But the criteria of our particularity as individuals are not the criteria of sameness as regards our claims. The result of so thinking, is, among other things, solipsism.

To establish the sameness of the two utterances, Mi and My, it is not necessary that I do your hearing or your seeing for you. Sufficiently similar conditions could be met without this requirement. Nor, in making the same M-claim as you was I in principle forever limited to less than optimum similar conditions, limited, that is, to less than your conditions. I could open the door to your house. But there was no further unopenable door beyond which lay those sufficiently similar conditions to be had only by you.

Similarly, your P-ascription to another, Py, is not in principle limited to your observations *of* another any more than My utterances are forever limited to conditions insufficiently similar to the utterance of an Mi statement. I was not necessarily limited to your reports about the tea party, nor to what was available to me only on this side of the door. Similarly, our ultimate and sufficient resource in making Py utterances is not observation of others but placing *ourselves* under the precise conditions in which the Pi statement was made by another. Nothing more is possible in *any* area of discourse, M or P, and thus the complaint that more is not possible in one of these areas does not distinguish it.

I think we are now in a position to say the following. We may accept the impersonal idiom as a case of the non-paradoxical. This seems safe ground since we could argue in defence of it that the sceptic could not outflank this non-paradoxical holding without losing the issue himself more quickly than otherwise. Were he, however, to attempt this maneuver and not accept that our impersonal discourse, our talk about things other than ourselves, is sceptic-proof, even as such utterances change person, then he would be on the road to solipsism. And once there his arguments had no weight.

We could expect then that if the sceptic had a case at all the purported shift-in-person difficulties among our personal predicates would *not* be re-constructable within our impersonal idiom. It seemed to me that they were, however, so duplicable if we accepted our P-utterances as a measure of the paradoxical. Actually it only appeared that such reconstruction was possible within our impersonal concepts; the insertion of sufficiently similar circumstances showed the case to be a fabrication among our M-predicates. But it also showed the shift-in-person case to be a fabricated difficulty within even our most personal utterances. Conditions of sufficient similarity were available in *both* M- and P-cases of ascription, and such conditions demonstrate the lack of a principled gap between first-person and other-person evidence in both types of case. This allows a *bona fide* use for both, 'I have the same basis as you for this M-ascription, for I hear, feel, touch, weigh, exactly what you do, am in just your circumstances', and, 'I have the same basis as you for this P-ascription for I am undergoing just what you are, am in just your circumstances.'

The penalty of denying the person-neutrality or person-universaliz*ability* of our P-ascriptions was, we saw, incoherence. That seemed to follow since there was nothing to prevent such denial covering M-cases too so that we ended in scepticism-without-contrast or complete solipsism; and so on. Contrariwise, to affirm that all of our predicates, M- and P-, are person-neutral means that we do accept the operative possibility of sufficiently similar circumstances among persons as well as things; i.e., we accept criteria of similarity and of qualitative identity.

And this is finally all we need to defeat the sceptic. Naturally, what he is exactly sceptical of is the availability of such criteria of similarity. But the pure suggestion of their *un*availability in every case, was incoherent. A more sophisticated sceptic might seem to avoid this by suggesting that criteria of qualitative identity were unavailable in only some, the personal cases. But then criteria for similarity among personal cases would be presupposed in such a sceptic's own acceptance of criteria in M-cases since the cases were too similar to support such a difference. Actually the only sceptic who does not seem gratuitously to deny criteria for similarity of conditions of the use of P-predicates among persons is the stringent solipsist; and we have seen that his 'too lonely I' is the easiest case to defeat.

The more sophisticated sceptic tries to limit his case to the shift-in-person aspect: only *some* first-person ascriptions have available a different basis for their utterance from those available to their second or third-person forms. But, he admits, there are also available some untroublesome similarities between selves and others, such as our material, or M-properties. The important question is: why should he say that *any* first-person utterance has available a *different* basis? Suppose, as we can (Section 18), we force the sceptic to admit that our first-personal bases for ascription, yours, mine, and his, are similar under similar conditions. We all feel our pain in the same way. Our sceptic then will have criteria for similarity and difference of our first-person bases of ascription. Otherwise he is not our sceptic. Otherwise he could not say whether his own basis was either similar to or different from your own basis or my own basis of self-ascription of P-predicates. That too would lead to a too unique use of P-predicates in the first-person. There is, however, meant to be a gap between us not as first-persons but only as first- and other-persons. But *this* shift-in-person gap could now only be contingent. Once I am assured that our first-person bases of P-ascription are similar under similar conditions then I close as well the gap between a self- and an other-ascription by satisfying the conditions of just such similarity: I place myself, where possible, under your circumstances: We become, as it were, the same grammatical person.

In short, if 'self' is allowed a necessary plural and hence conditions for similarity among first-person uses of our P-predicates, then these same conditions close the gap between oneself and another. I have suggested that these conditions of similarity are physical conditions of the body, environment, history, and so on.

It is also true that the more sophisticated sceptic both accepts and denies conditions for similarity for P-ascription. He accepts them insofar as he claims that there is more than one self, more than one legitimate user of 'I'; he accepts sufficiently similar conditions among first-persons when he holds there is similarity of grounds among self-ascribers of P-properties. But he denies the function of these same sufficiently similar circumstances which assure us that similar self-ascribers have similar experiences *when he makes it more than a contingent fact that we are limited in our other-ascriptions to something short of what we have available in our self-predications of P-states.* When we other-ascribe P-states we are not, however, limited to just what we may see or hear of another: we may in principle ourselves undergo just that P-state: we become first-person too and under just your first-person conditions.

I have argued that P-ascription is not more of a problem than M-ascription as they each relate to the shift-in person-case. I do, however, want to admit that there is a difference between M- and P-cases across that shift and that this difference may be why, or partly why, we do distinguish M- from P-ascriptions.

In the matter of sight, for instance, we are not troubled by the shift-in-person case. In normal circumstances if you see x, I may see x by doing the appropriate things. We may indeed *both* see x, the same x. It is because there is a legitimate sense to this last statement that I may be assured that you see what I see and that I see what you see. We have criteria of identity for visual objects and these criteria are shift-in-person-neutral. They are person-neutral because we think (find) that sufficiently similar conditions produce sufficiently similar results. And individual persons seem, physically, sufficiently similar in most cases to be discounted as anything but a constant factor in the, say, visual situation. Our language functions on the premiss, well backed-up that we are sufficiently similar to each other to be reckoned discountable constants within the use of the language. The same premiss holds for physical objects. Similar objects will behave similarly – that is indeed at least a necessary condition of their similarity – hence many of our descriptions, experiments, etc., may be change-in-object-neutral.

Why, however, *should* we have supposed that while I could see exactly what you see, it was problematic whether I could feel what you felt. I felt what I felt but could only see or hear that you felt so. Why should we have supposed that I must have different evidence that you felt from that which I had for my own case?

In some instances it is more difficult than others to muster the sufficiently similar conditions for me to experience what you do. In cases of sight, touch, sound, taste, smell, it is often quite simple. If we are present together at the same time that will often suffice. In cases of sympathy, humiliation, jealousy, love, hate, tiredness, jubilation, and the like, more is required. Merely being together in the presence of a particular object mostly won't do for these cases. The replication of circumstances sufficiently similar could be an enormously difficult chore – or even impossible for a particular individual, given what may have already passed for him. In these cases we tend to rely more heavily upon sense modes which have been already legitimately co-related with these P-cases. I see that you are jubilant, rather than feel your jubilance; but I, or someone, could conceivably do either. That your actual jubilance may be felt by someone else is the ground of our ability to non-sceptically co-relate that feeling with certain antecedent and consequent events and hence also to establish and trust a verbal convention. That is why we may non-sceptically, but still derivatively, see and hear, or be told, that you are jubilant. The tendency and need to trust such co-related behavior is much more powerful, I want to say, in P-cases. This is so because we rarely have the time or resources to duplicate for ourselves your relevant P-conditions: they are often much too complex and deviant. And often they involve too much of the history of the individual. But, luckily, we need not always duplicate your P-conditions in order to P-ascribe to you. We have the shorter circuit of trusting your co-related and conventional behavior and other events. On the other hand, for me to see what you see I often need only look at what you have looked at. (Of course here too I could, say, see that you see rather than see what you see.) The reproduction of similar conditions is often a simple matter where our histories to that point are not relevantly deviant. Compare the conditions which might have to be met in Enos in order for him to love Paul's mother as does Paul, with the conditions to be met in order for Enos merely to hear what Paul hears from Paul's wife.

P-conditions of similarity are, as a rule, much less readily available to us than are M-conditions. Should we forget the contingent reasons for this and feel that we must in one case rely solely upon another's behavior and M-state in order to ascribe to him a P-state, while in the other we are not so circumscribed, sceptical consequences are possible; and so are odd solutions. Type-distinct consequences might also seem to follow if we forget what underwrites our acceptance of another's behavior and M-state as a true indication of how he feels. When we remember that our reliance on another's behavior and M-state is only a contingent reliance in second and third person P-cases, certainly scepticism is not consequent; neither is the need for a type-distinction between M- and P-predicates – at least not upon these antecedents.

It need not be the intention of this or other parts of my argument to show that there is no principle which might distinguish M- from P-utterances, no principle which might distinguish persons from things. Indeed, I think I have just shown one. What I have tried to suggest in this last section is that the notion of sufficiently similar circumstances allows us to close the gap, usually reported, between the self-ascription and the other-ascription of P-predicates. The availability of sufficiently similar circumstances, I would want to hold, leaves P-discourse in as unproblematic a state as M-discourse, its necessary and usual contrast. What is secondarily suggested is that no credit is to be given arguments which make capital out of such purported asymmetries, epistemic and otherwise, between our personal and our impersonal discourse. But the acceptance of some such asymmetry has been the history of the Philosophy of Mind.

Selected Bibliography

JP–Journal of Philosophy
M–Mind
P–Philosophy
PASS–Proceedings of the Aristotalian Society, Supplementary Volume
PQ–Philosophical Quarterly
PR–Philosophical Review

Austin, J., 'Other Minds', *PASS*, XX (1946).

Austin, J., 'Pretending', *PASS*, XXXII (1958).

Ayer, A. J., *The Concept of a Person*, Macmillan, 1963.

Feigl, H., 'Other Minds and the Egocentric Predicament', *JP*, LV (1958).

Grice, P., 'The Causal Theory of Perception', *PASS*, XXXV (1961).

Grice, P., 'Some Remarks About the Senses', *Analytical Philosophy*, ed. R. J. Butler, Blackwell, 1962.

Lucas, John, 'Minds Machines and Gödel', *P*, XXXVI (1961).

Malcom, Norman, 'Knowledge of Other Minds', *JP*, LV (1958).

Pears, D. F., '*Individuals* by P. F. Strawson', *PQ*, XI (1961).

Pears, D. F., 'Dreaming', *M*, LXX (1961).

Place, U. T., 'Is Consciousness a Brain Process?', *British Journal of Psychology*, XLVII (1956).

Putnam, Hilary, 'Minds and Machines', *Dimensions of Mind*, ed. S. Hook, N.Y., 1960.

Putnam, Hilary, 'Dreaming and Depth Grammar', *Analytical Philosophy*, ed. R. J. Butler, Blackwell, 1962.

Putnam, Hilary, 'Brains and Behaviour', *Analytical Philosophy* (2), ed. R. J. Butler, Blackwell, 1964.

Shoemaker, S., *Self Knowledge and Self Identity*, Cornell University Press, 1963.

Smart, J. J. C., 'Sensations and Brain Processes', *PR*, LXVIII (1959).

Smart, J. J. C., *Philosophy and Physical Realism*, Routledge and Kegan Paul, 1963.

Strawson, P. F., *Individuals*, Methuen, 1959.

Wisdom, John, *Other Minds*, Blackwell, 1952.

Wittgenstein, L., *Philosophical Investigations*, Blackwell, 1953.